Defrocking the Supreme Court

Also by Jake Highton

Reporter
Editing
The Spirit That Says No
Nevada Newspaper Days
Against the Mainstream
Saying Nay
No! In Thunder
Disdaining Lies
Disobedience & Rebellion
Facing the Truth
Truths Are Treason
Speaking the Truth
Everlasting No
No!
Wrong
A Terrible Country
In League with the Future
Standing Alone
I Dissent
Shame the Devil
You Speak Treason

Defrocking the Supreme Court

Jake Highton

*Emeritus journalism professor
at the University of Nevada, Reno.*

Reno, Nevada

Sketch by Jennifer Klein of the Sparks Tribune.

Cover: photos of Chief Justice John Roberts and the Supreme Court Plaza. Source: Wikipedia.

World Vision Publishing
© 2015 by World Vision Publishing. All rights reserved
Printed in United States of America
10 09 08 07 06   15 14 13 12 11 10 9

Library of Congress Catalog Card Number: 2014922077
Highton, Jake
A Collection of Newspaper Columns

ISBN (10) 0-9727173-4-x
ISBN (13) 9780972717342

The problem with the Supreme Court is that the justices are lawyers. That is not a nightclub comedian's joke. It's a searing truth.

Lawyers are legalistic rather than humanistic. They are narrow-minded rather than broad-minded. They favor corporations rather than consumers.

Most federal judges are rich. In two terms President Reagan appointed 279 U.S. judges. The majority had a net worth of $400,000. One fifth of them were millionaires. Such judges are unlikely to favor ordinary people.

The great socialist leader Eugene Debs pointed out that a member of the working class has never been on the federal bench let alone on the august Supreme Court.

Most justices have been mediocrities. President Washington named 10 justices, "a thoroughly undistinguished lot," Peter Irons wrote in "A People's History of the Supreme Court."

Jake Highton

Contents

On Roberts Court Rulings..........................3
More Woeful Decisions 65
Worst Supreme Court Decisions...........137
Magnificent Dissents..............................147

On Roberts Court Rulings

Judicial politicians rule court

The Founding Fathers intended America to be a country in which every citizen has the inalienable right to donate $3.6 million to politicians.
>Gail Collins in a sardonic comment in her New York Times column

The Supreme Court is still doing its dirty work. It doesn't interpret the law. It makes it, contrary to the Constitution that gives that job to Congress.

Because of its recent decision in the McCutcheon case, political spending is now unlimited. The court struck down sensible congressional efforts to limit the noisome influence of money in politics.

As a result, legalized bribery continues to reign supreme in politics. The five flagrantly partisan Republicans commanding the supreme bench handed down the decree.

The decision, dubbed Citizens United II after the 2010 Supreme Court ruling prohibiting government from restricting political expenditures, means corporations and big business win again. It means that America is an oligarchy--rule of the few.

Blatant capitalism by judicial usurpers has become the hallmark of the Roberts Court.

Brendan Fischer, writing an analysis for Truthout, observed accurately: "Because of the McCutcheon decision, the handful of millionaires and billionaires can now dole out $3.6 million per election cycle among candidates and committees."

Chief Justice Roberts is the leader of the band of usurpers. His major opinions are Jesuitical: deceptive, misleading and disingenuous. They are also intellectually dishonest. The other usurpers are Justices Scalia, Thomas, Kennedy and Alito.

Mike Lofgren, wrote a scathing editorial on Truthout about the four other usurpers: "Scalia, the opinionated blowhard at your local saloon; Thomas, the total cipher; Alito, the professional Catholic who might have come from the curia in Rome; and Kennedy, the guy who is purportedly the swing vote but whose mind is already made up."

Anatole France wonderfully exemplified Roberts' legal casuistry: "The law, in its majestic equality, forbids the rich as well as the poor to sleep under bridges, to beg in the streets and to steal bread."

Moreover, the Reverend Roberts took 88 pages to deliver the pious sermon in his McCutcheon opinion:

"There is no right more basic in our democracy than the right to participate in electing our political leaders... Money in politics may at times seem repugnant to some but so does much of what the First Amendment vigorously protects. If it protects flag burning, funeral protests and American Nazi parades, it surely protects political campaign speech."

In short, money is free speech. No one has more reverence for the First Amendment than this columnist. But curbing the amount of money in politics hardly erodes the Mighty First.

Justice Breyer, in a dissenting opinion signed by Justices Ginsburg, Sotomayor and Kagan, denounced the Roberts fiat:

"It is wrong. Its conclusion rests on its own, not a record-based view of the facts. Its legal analysis is faulty. It misconstrues the nature of the competing constitutional issues at stake.

"It understates the importance of protecting the political integrity of governmental institutions. It creates a loophole that will allow a single individual to contribute millions of dollars to a political party or to a candidate's campaign.

"Taken together with Citizens United v. Federal Election Commission, the decision eviscerates our nation's campaign finance laws, leaving a remnant incapable of dealing with the grave problems of democratic legitimacy that those laws were intended to resolve."

Some editorial writers, ignorant of the math involved, have proposed a constitutional amendment to take the money out of politics. Never happen.

Constitutional amendments first must be approved by a supermajority of two-thirds vote in each house of Congress. A hard number to achieve. Even harder is the next step: approval by a super-supermajority of three-fourths of the states. This means just 13 states can defeat any proposed constitutional amendment.

The Roberts Court personifies the point of a letter written by an attorney to the San Francisco Chronicle: "After practicing law for 40 years, I've observed that when judges want to get a certain result they have no more honesty than a used-car salesman."

The five pols, abandoning any pretense at justice, produced the result they wanted.

Sparks Tribune, April 24, 2014

Absurd court rulings pile up

No woman can call herself free who does not own and control her body.

Margaret Sanger

The Supreme Court ended its term with a reactionary bang, five male Catholic justices declaring that corporations do not have to provide contraceptive insurance to employees because it violates their religious freedom.

That Hobby Lobby decision, ignoring women's right to use contraceptives, was typical of Roberts Court rulings on most important issues: pro-business and pro-wealth, anti-poor and anti-people and Republican and reprehensible.

Chief Justice Roberts and Justices Scalia, Thomas, Kennedy and Alito handed down the 5-4 ruling of the outrageously biased court. As dissenting Justice Breyer, himself a Catholic, phrased it: "junior varsity politicians motivated by partisan agendas better left to elected officials."

The Roberts Court's most outrageous political decisions have included making campaign money speech in Citizen's United I and II (McCutcheon), rulings that have made the Supremes the butt of talk show hosts.

Alito wrote a nonsensical opinion for the zealous fundamentalists, declaring falsely that "the effect of the ruling on women employed by Hobby Lobby and other companies would be precisely zero."

The court continues the horrible pattern: corporations are people and money in politics is free speech that gives the rich a far greater First Amendment than four people out of a million have. Campaign bribery by the wealthy is legal.

Never mind the wise view of retired Justice Stevens that "corporations have no consciences, no beliefs, no feelings and no thoughts." Their sole desire is to make heaps of money.

Brian Burghart, editor of the Reno News & Review, puts it perfectly: "The Supreme Court chooses money over human dignity."

Justice Ginsburg had it right in a powerful dissent joined by Justices Sotomayor, Kagan and Breyer: "The court forgets that religious organizations exist to serve a community of believers. For-profit corporations do not fit that bill."

She attacked the majority opinion as "a radical overhaul of corporate rights," one that applies to all corporations and to numerous laws.

Her opinion cited the Guttmacher Institute, a research and policy group, which pointed out that many women cannot afford effective means of birth control and that insurance coverage reduces unintended pregnancies and hence the need for abortions.

Hobby Lobby, which operates a chain of arts and crafts stores, is pervasively Christian, playing evangelical music while its stores are open all week except Sunday.

It is also pervasively hypocritical. It does a huge business with China, a nation that forces women to have abortions. It invests $73 million of employee pension money in mutual funds that include companies making contraceptive pills and IUDs.

In a case related to Hobby Lobby, the Roberts Court struck down the 35-foot protective area around abortion clinic entrances in Massachusetts under the guise of the First Amendment.

The buffer zones were rightly established because of anti-abortionist threats to public safety--harassment, intimidation of workers and a history of violent protests. In 1994 two Planned Parenthood workers were murdered.

In another outrageous ruling (Harris v. Quinn), the five

retrograde justices overturned an Illinois law requiring workers not wishing to join the union to pay a "fair share" of the cost of collective bargaining and union representation.

Again the reactionaries trotted out the First Amendment to rationalize their decision. The mighty First has nothing to do with "free riders," workers getting the benefits of union representation without paying for them. The court's next step doubtless is to imbed nefarious right-to-work laws in constitutional law.

Earlier this term, the court ruled that town boards may start their meetings with prayer, a clear violation of the cherished separation of church and state. It also upheld a Michigan voter affirmative action law banning the taking of race into account for admission to universities--a blatant refusal to admit that racism still exists in America.

Even when the Roberts Court showed a modicum of wisdom when it ruled that a Florida I.Q. law was too rigid in capital punishment cases, it indulged in halfwayism. The Eighth Amendment prohibition of "cruel and unusual punishments" clearly makes the death penalty unconstitutional.

The Roberts Court did hand down two progressive decisions this term, striking down Virginia's ban on gay marriage and declaring that cellphone searches require a warrant.

But the sad reality remains in most cases: justices are lawyers, which means that most justices are conservatives whose aim in life is to make money. As James Madison wrote in No. 63 of the Federalist Papers, they "abuse liberty as well as power."

Sparks Tribune, July 17, 2014

Court clings to woeful ruling

Republicans rule the retrograde House because of the misguided voting of the American people, the Senate because of the unconstitutional filibuster and the Supreme Court because of reactionary political decisions.

Democracy is a huge loser in all three cases.

The disastrous Supreme Court decision of Citizens United in 2010, equating money with speech, gave the superrich a far greater First Amendment than nearly all Americans have.

What the decision means was illustrated just the other day: the Koch brothers and their fellow money barons will spend $400 million in private money to defeat President Obama this fall.

The amount, unprecedented in American political history, is no one's idea of democracy except for the five-man majority of the Supreme Court.

Given an opportunity to reverse Citizens United the court again repudiated democracy.

The court Monday summarily struck down a decision by the Montana Supreme Court that had upheld a state law limiting political spending by corporations.

The opinion was unsigned by the Gutless Five: Chief Justice Roberts and Justices Scalia, Thomas, Kennedy and Alito.

The court did not have the courtesy and judicial wisdom to hold oral arguments and let briefs be submitted. Such legal necessities could have shown just how outrageous Citizens United is.

It is arbitrary and impertinent to decide a case without adequate information and deliberation. Sadly, such a tactic is typical of the Republican court presided over by Roberts.

No means no, the court said in effect. It said Citizens United clearly "applies to the Montana state law."

But in dissent for the liberal bloc of four, Justice Stephen Breyer declared that Citizens United was a mistake, that it was wrong for the court to have assumed "independent expenditures do not corrupt."

"Given the history and political landscape in Montana, the state court had a compelling interest in limiting expenditures by corporations," Breyer declared.

Mike McGrath, chief justice of the Montana court, stressed in his opinion that state politics had been corrupted by corporate interests so the law was justified.

"Montana had been operating under a mere shell of legal authority and the real social and political power was wielded by powerful corporate managers to further their own business interests," McGrath wrote.

The state's "copper kings," who controlled a huge chunk of the state's wealth, blatantly bribed legislators.

A New York Times editorial summed up the Supreme Court ruling: the retrograde majority "turned itself into a copper kings' court."

Foes of Citizens United and some legal authorities urge a constitutional amendment to foil a clearly partisan court. But the math of that is prohibitive. It explains why a constitutional amendment to reverse Citizens United is most unlikely.

A constitutional amendment requires a super majority of two-thirds vote in each house of Congress before approval of the states is sought. A high hurdle indeed!

But an even higher hurdle: three-fourths of the states must ratify the proposed amendment. That means 38 states, an awesome number.

(The Constitution can be changed by constitutional convention but precious few want to take that route. A convention would pose a dire threat to American civil liberties embodied by the Constitution's Bill of Rights.)

As for Montana, it has one of the most transparent democracies in the world.

Its governor, Brian Schweitzer, has an open-door policy for all Montanans. As he says, "I'm just a rancher"--like many others in the state.

In an op-edit column in the Times, Schweitzer eloquently told why Montana insisted on keeping corporate money out of politics.

"A miner named William Clark came upon a massive copper vein near Butte," he wrote. "It was the largest deposit on earth. Overnight he became one of the wealthiest men in the world.

"He bought up half the state of Montana. If he needed favors from politicians he bought those as well.

"In 1899 he wanted to become a U.S. senator. (State legislatures then appointed U.S. senators.) Clark simply gave each corruptible lawmaker $10,000."

So Clark became a U.S. senator. But the Senate soon kicked him out when it learned of the bribes. This caused the bought-and-paid-for senator to rightfully complain that he "never bought a man who wasn't for sale."

Schweitzer concluded that the Clark case prompted Montana citizens to approve a ballot initiative banning corporate money from campaigns.

Today large campaign contributions are legalized bribery, a political corruption twice sanctioned by the Supreme Court.

No wonder so many American citizens have lost faith in this so-called democracy.

Sparks Tribune, July 17, 2014

Supremes ignorant of gay marriage

The Supreme Court justices are wandering in the Dark Ages on gay marriage, cloistered in their ivory tower, isolated from real people in the real world.

During recent oral arguments the justices showed gross ignorance of the subject, its history and the long struggle for gay and lesbian equality.

Justice Alito complained that "same-sex marriage was very new." He apparently never heard of the Stonewall riots, a series of demonstrations in 1969 by gays against a police raid at the Stonewall Inn in New York City's Greenwich Village.

It was the beginning of the gay liberation movement like the beginning of women's liberation at Seneca Falls, N.Y., in 1848 and the beginning of black liberation at Selma, Ala., in 1965.

Many justices seemed unaware that the term gay has long been used instead of homosexual. Some spoke of the "sanctity of marriage," oblivious of the fact that 50 percent of marriages end in divorce.

The saddest aspect of the oral arguments was the right-wing views of two usual liberals, Justices Ginsburg and Sotomayor. Their queasiness was dumbfounding.

"We let issues perk and so we let racial segregation perk for 56 years from 1898 to 1954," Sotomayor said. Perk? An absurdity. Fifty-six years is much too long to end injustice. Sotomayor uttered more nonsense about the states and society needing more time "to figure out" its stance on gay marriage.

She too was sleeping like Rip Van Winkle through the whole same-sex marriage controversy. Ginsburg, while approving the Roe decision, has lectured constantly that the abortion issue "moved too far, too fast." More nonsense from a justice who should know better.

While the reactionary Scalia railed about the "possible destructive effects" of gay couples adopting children, Justice Kennedy rightly observed that "40,000 children in California living with gay parents want their parents to have full recognition and status."

Yet Kennedy wrongly argued for the right of states to regulate marriage. Gay marriage is a constitutional matter, not something that should be made law by political cretins in state legislatures and by retrograde state voters.

California voters decided in Proposition 8 to ban gay marriage. It was a perfect example of the public being wrong. Columnist Maureen Dowd of the New York Times zeroed in on the problem: "civil rights should not hinge on the whims of the people."

And The Nation columnist Melissa Harris-Perry pointed to another truth: "For decades LGBT (gay, lesbian, bisexual and transgender) people have had families built on commitment, love and parental devotion. Moreover, marriage equality will extend a basic civil right and allow LGBT Americans to get the economic protections associated with matrimony."

They deserve all those rights.

Take the case of Edie Windsor of New York. When her female married partner died the law did not allow the IRS to treat her as a surviving spouse as it would have for a husband. She was assessed a tax bill of $363,000 for inheritance of her partner's estate.

As for the Defense of Marriage Act (DOMA), it is indefensible. Justice Kagan noted the act was passed by Congress out of "dislike, animus and fear."

Whatever the court rules in June, the battle is already won. Respondents to a nationwide poll recently said they approved of gay marriage 58 to 36 percent. The margin was wider among young people: 81 percent. Even right-wing kook Rush Limbaugh admitted "the issue is lost."

Roberts indulged in legalisms that skirted the issue. He questioned whether the people challenging Proposition 8 had standing (the right to sue). He expressed irritation that the issue was before the court. He argued fatuously that the institution of marriage "didn't include homosexual couples."

President Clinton, the gutless wonder, shamefully signed the DOMA under the cover of darkness in 1996. He admitted recently his regret at signing the bill. The truth is he feared backlash in an election year.

The law was wrong then as it is now. But as they often do, presidents act for political reasons rather than humanity.

Sparks Tribune, April 25, 2013

Court kills Voting Rights Act

After practicing law for 40 years I've observed that when judges want to get a certain result they have no more honesty than a used-car salesman.
        Richard Covert, letter to San Francisco Chronicle

Supreme Court Chief Justice Roberts is a master of Jesuitical opinions: deceptive, misleading, subtle, sly, crafty--and specious.

Roberts is also skillful at persuading liberal justices to join his opinions. But don't you be fooled: he is a right-wing partisan.

The result is an ever more reactionary court masked by Robert's seeming reasonableness. His opinions are often wrong but few people see it. The former Justice David Souter did. He loathed Roberts for his "disrespect of precedent, his grasping conservatism and his aggressive pursuit of political objectives."

Nevertheless, Roberts rules the court if he can get swingman Justice Kennedy to join his three other exponents of reaction: Justices Scalia, Thomas and Alito.

In the 2012-2013 term just concluded the court continued to be good for business. It showered the Chamber of Commerce with victories:

Cutting back on class actions suits that are essential for fairness to "the little guy"; making it harder to sue the makers of dangerous drugs; favoring employers in workplace discrimination; limiting suits against corporations for human rights abuses abroad; and allowing companies to avoid class-actions suits through arbitration agreements.

A perfect example of Roberts' workmanship: his opinion stabbing the heart of the historic Voting Rights Act (VRA) of 1965.

Judiciary theorist Richard Posner is merciless. He calls it: "a lame piece of work," offering weak support and a "newly invented 'fundamental principle of equal sovereignty.' " Posner concludes: "It simply does not wash."

"Voting discrimination still exists," Roberts wrote. "No one doubts that. The question is whether the act's extraordinary measures, including the disparate treatment of the states, continue to satisfy constitutional requirements."

They do not, the retrograde court ruled, 5-4. Eight states in the South are free to change election laws without U.S. approval. They are free to keep blacks from the polls with voter ID, raise barriers to early voting and to carve out discriminatory voting districts.

Roberts, living in the court's dream world, says the VRA law is "based on 40-year-old facts having no relationship to the present day." Justice Scalia is also living in that fantasy world, calling the law during oral argument a "perpetuation of racial entitlement." In other words, giving blacks something they don't deserve.

The Roberts decision was "intellectually dishonest and disingenuous," as the New York Times pointed out.

Justice Ginsburg cried out in an angry dissent joined by Justice Breyer, Kagan and Sotomayor: "Hubris is a fit word for today's demolition of VRA. The sad irony of the decision lies in its utter failure to grasp why the VRA has proven effective. The court errs egregiously.

"Early attempts to cope with this vile infection resembled battling the Hydra. Whenever one form of voting discrimination was prohibited, others sprang up in its place.

"When confronting the most constitutionally invidious form of discrimination and the most fundamental right in our democratic system, Congress's power to act is at its height.

"The Constitution vests broad powers in Congress to protect the right to vote and in particular to combat racial discrimination in voting. This court has repeatedly reaffirmed Congress' prerogative to use any rational means in exercise of its power in this area."

The Ginsburg dissent was long but necessary to express her anguish. She cited the Fifteenth Amendment ratified in 1870: "The right of citizens of the United States to vote shall not be denied or abridged by the Untied States or any state on account of race, color or previous condition of servitude."

Ginsburg was absolutely right. But ideology reigns in the Roberts court, not reason. Roberts and his fellow politicians, Scalia, Thomas, Alito and Kennedy, make the law.

Judges are supposed to be impartial. But whatever wrong ruling they hand down they always muster arguments for it. Roberts is very good at it--to the detriment of the nation.

This columnist refers to the Supremes as the Roberts court. But perhaps Dennis Myers, news editor of the Reno News & Review, is more perceptive. He refers to them as the Kennedy court.

In any case, Greg Palast of Truthout was so incensed by the VRA ruling that he called it the "Ku Klux Kourt," figuratively dancing on the grave of Martin Luther King. As cartoonist Garry Trudeau in Doonesbury puts it: "the return of Jimmy Crow" allows voter suppression.

It's a subtle form of apartheid 148 years after the Civil War ended.

Sparks Tribune, July 11, 2013

Gays slowly climb mountain

Scarcely any political question arises in the United States which is not resolved, sooner or later, into a judicial question.

     Tocqueville, "Democracy in America," 1835

 The lower federal courts have spoken: California's Proposition 8 banning gay marriage is invalid. But that's hardly definitive. The Supreme Court decides the law of the land.

 U.S. Judge Vaughn Walker of the Northern District of California ruled in 2010 that Proposition 8 was unconstitutional. The 9th U.S. Circuit Court of Appeals recently agreed. So the 9th Circuit ruling appears to be headed to the highest court for final adjudication.

 There the portent may not be good.

 The 9th Circuit, the most liberal court in the land, is often overturned by the reactionary high court. It could do so again if "the past is the future."

 Judge Stephen Reinhardt, who wrote the 9th Circuit majority opinion, is one of the most progressive judges in America. Unfortunately, the five controlling justices at the Supreme Court are some of the worst judges in America.

 If the Supreme Court accepts the case, gay marriage could go down. The court's Retrograde Five seldom rules for compassion and modernism.

 Yet there are exceptions so there is reason to hope.

 In 2003 one of the five reactionaries, Justice Anthony Kennedy, stunned court watchers by joining the liberal bloc to strike down state sodomy laws (Lawrence v. Texas).

 Kennedy could do so again on gay marriage.

 In Lawrence, the majority of justices realized that gays and lesbians deserve "respect for their private lives" and "freedom from government intrusion in their bedrooms,"

Kennedy wrote. "Times can blind us to certain truths and later generations can see that laws once thought necessary served only to oppress."

Or, as Justice Holmes put it more succinctly, "the law responds to the felt necessities of our time."

Proposition 8 was approved in 2008 by the voters of California--7 million of them. But that hardly makes it right. It is an example of tyranny of the majority. They voted their moral judgment rather than for justice.

Judge Walker was emphatic: "Proposition 8 cannot withstand scrutiny of the equal protection clause... Fundamental rights may not be submitted to a vote...The Constitution cannot control private biases but neither can it tolerate them."

Nor did Judge Reinhardt mince words: "Proposition 8 lessens the status and human dignity of gays and lesbians. It classifies their relationships as inferior to those of opposite-sex couples."

Meanwhile, legislation statewide slowly advances *la causa*. The governor of Washington signed a bill this week making Washington the seventh state to approve gay marriage.

But there's still a huge mountain to climb, prejudice and violence to overcome.

Gay, lesbian, bisexual and transgender people around the world face bias, abuse and violence, including torture and rape.

A recent United Nations report said members of sexual minorities are subject to attack by "religious extremists, paramilitary groups, neo-Nazis and extreme nationalists." These heinous assaults often end in mutilation and castration.

Secretary of State Hillary Clinton is on the side if the angels in the fight for LGBT human rights.

She made these powerful points in a December speech in Geneva:

• Being gay is not some Western invention but "a human reality."

• Religious and cultural values do not justify criminal attacks against LGBTs.

• People are free to believe what they want but they are not free to deny a group's humanity.

Another gay-lesbian advance long overdue: the military abolition of its heinous policy of "don't ask, don't tell."

Some 13,000 military men and women have been fired since the policy was adopted in 1993 in a fit of righteous furor. The ill-advised policy discharged much-needed linguists and intelligence analysts while unjustly depriving all of careers.

Kate Kendell, head of the National Center for Lesbian Rights based in San Francisco, was jubilant.

"We are within sight of a time when LGBT people can participate in all aspects of society without fear of being singled out for stigma and discrimination by their own government," Kendell said.

And in December the 11th U.S. Circuit Court of Appeals (Atlanta) ruled that transgender people are entitled to equal protection under the 14th Amendment.

The Supreme Court ruled in 1959 that interracial marriage, illegal in the apartheid South, was unconstitutional. But in Alabama the Constitution be damned. It took until 2000 for that racist state to repeal the vestige of Jim Crow.

Yes, the fight for equality is long and arduous in America.

Sparks Tribune, Feb. 19, 2012

Stevens book misfires

SIX AMENDMENTS
How and Why We Should Change the Constitution
By John Paul Stevens
133 pages plus Constitution, Little Brown, 2014

John Paul Stevens has written a slim book with a huge aim: amending the Constitution. But chances of ratification of his proposals are nil. The math of amending the Constitution is forbidding.

Stevens, a former member of the Supreme Court, should know better. The Constitution has been amended just 27 times in 215 years.

The first Congress passed 10 amendments, mostly important ones contained in the Bill of Rights, including the magnificent First Amendment guaranteeing freedom of speech and religion. Three other amendments dealt with liberated slaves: abolishing involuntary servitude, making Negroes citizens and granting them the right to vote.

Four important amendments gave women the right to vote, allowed 18 year olds to vote, abolished the poll tax and established a federal income tax. The Prohibition amendment was wisely abolished by a subsequent amendment. And some were mere perfecting amendments like having candidates for president and vice president run on the same ticket.

Proposed constitutional amendments rarely succeed unless they are pressing issues with wide support. Most proposals do not have the immense backing necessary.

Constitutional amendments first must be approved by a supermajority of two-thirds vote in each house of Congress. A hard number to achieve. Even harder is the next step: approval by a super-supermajority of three-fourths of the states. This means just 13 states can defeat any proposed amendment. (State conventions can also amend the Constitution but are rarely used.)

As for the Stevens book, it is often tedious and covers far too many cases that are irrelevant to his proposals.

"I am confident the soundness of each of my proposals will become more and more evident and that ultimately each will be adopted," he writes. His confidence is overinflated. They will not be ratified--not even in 200 years.

Here are his proposals:

• Stevens would add "and other public officials" to the Supremacy Clause in Article VI. This is an arcane matter, too technical and unimportant to anyone not specializing in the Constitution.

• He rightly condemns gerrymandering, the drawing of voting districts for partisan political gain. This leads to bizarre configurations, some districts looking like snakes. Stevens wants to mandate a constitutional change to make districts "compact and composed of contiguous territory."

Never happen. Politicians want to gerrymander. They may be on the "losing" side now but when they gain control they will gerrymander too.

• Stevens proposes an amendment that would allow Congress and state legislatures to limit political campaign spending. Fine idea. But the Supreme Court has ruled three times that money is speech and under the First Amendment cannot be limited (Buckley v. Valeo, Citizens United and, since Stevens wrote the book, McCutcheon).

Senate Majority Leader Harry Reid backs a constitutional amendment to limit campaign spending, aiming for a Senate vote in July. Good. The reactionary Supreme Court rulings should be overturned. Money has nothing to do with free speech. However, hurdles to ratification are high.

• States, their agencies and officials would not have immunity from liability for violating an act of Congress.

Again much discussion about the arcane 10th and 11th amendments that few have ever heard about and even fewer care about.

• Stevens would add the words "such as the death penalty" to the Eighth Amendment forbidding "cruel and unusual punishment." Excellent idea. But the reality is something else. Just 18 states bar the death penalty--a long, long way from 34!

• Stevens rightly wants gun controls. "Each year 30,000 people die in the United States in firearm-related incidents," he notes. But the National Rifle Associations wants no controls of any kind. It stands by the badly outdated Second Amendment. What the NRA wants it gets--even sawed-off shotguns and machine guns for public use.

Board member Ted Nugent shows the lower depths of NRA thinking when he says of President Obama: "A Chicago communist-nurtured subhuman mongrel who weaseled his way into the top office in America."

Former Chief Justice Warren Burger had it right when he said: the Second Amendment defense is one of "the greatest frauds on the American public by special interest groups that I have ever seen."

The proposed constitutional changes, however well intentioned, have none of the great support necessary for ratification. Stevens might better have proposed making the amending process easier. That too would not be ratified but is a far worthier objective.

Sparks Tribune, May 22, 2014

Nation the real loser

The midterm election was a disaster, the Republicans seizing control of the Senate and increasing their majority in the House. The nation is the real loser.

Abandon all hope of getting even mildly liberal legislation passed by such reactionary troglodytes.

Nevertheless, immigration reform is now likely because President Obama has finally mustered the courage to issue an executive order granting legal status to millions of undocumented workers. He promises the order "soon."

Obama set a summer deadline for the order but refused to act under pressure from Senate Democrats who feared it would harm them in the mid-term election. It did. The clichéd saying is to be careful about what you wish for. The wish came true with a vengeance for the Dems.

Democratic President Harry Truman used to offer variations of this reality in his many speeches in the early 1950s.

"When the Democratic candidate starts apologizing for the New Deal and the Fair Deal and says he really doesn't believe in them, he is sure to lose," Truman said. "The people don't want a phony Democrat. If it's a choice between a genuine Republican and a Republican in Democratic clothing, the people will choose the genuine article."

George Lakoff in an op-ed for Truthout updated Truman's point: "The democratic strategists before the midterm election kept arguing for a move to the right. This left Democratic candidates without an authentic identity."

Regardless, the majority of voters failed to realize that the GOP is wrong about everything. It is wrong about immigration reform. It is wrong about climate control. It is wrong on the equal rights amendment for women. It is wrong opposing Obamacare--and that is not even the universal health care that all civilized countries have.

The most ominous development of the midterm election was the cascade of dark money into campaigns. As the New York Times phrased it in an editorial: "The next Senate was just elected on the greatest wave of secret, special-interest money ever raised in a congressional election."

The Supreme Court set the table for this dark money by permitting it in two recent decisions, Citizens United and McCutcheon. The Retrograde Five in the majority ruled that unlimited amounts of money could be spent in campaigns. In other words, buying elections.

Billionaires poured $4 million into campaigns, all of it hidden from public scrutiny.

It is legalized bribery.

Sparks Tribune, Nov. 18, 2014

Smug court rulings blasted

The Supreme Court has struck again, chopping down the nation's historic separation of church and state. The reactionary five dominating the Roberts Court ruled recently that the town of Greece in upstate New York can begin town hall meetings with a prayer by a Christian chaplain.

Justice Kennedy, hatchet man for the retrogrades, in his decision called such prayers "deeply embedded in the history and tradition of this country."

They certainly are. But that hardly makes them constitutional. The Supreme Court itself opens its public sessions unconstitutionally. The court marshal utters: "God save the United States and this honorable court."

Even if there were a God, it's a matter for houses of worship, not for invocation at public meetings. The First Amendment prohibits it.

Unfortunately, we will be stuck for at least a decade with the frightful adjudication of the Roberts Court. Moreover, there is nothing honorable about a court ruled by politicians.

Justice Kennedy said the prayers are ceremonial, "signaling the solemnity of the occasion, lending gravity and reflecting values long part of the nation's heritage." All of that too is unconstitutional nonsense, invented reasons to produce the outcome the five "good Catholics" wanted.

Some of the prayers are explicitly sectarian like the one referring to "the saving sacrifice of Jesus Christ on the cross." Yet Kennedy rambled on.

He said both houses of Congress have chaplains who start sessions with prayer. State legislatures begin with prayer, "a practice accepted by the Framers and withstanding critical scrutiny of time and political change."

Joining Kennedy were Chief Justice John Roberts and Justices Scalia, Thomas and Alito.

Justice Kagan dissented angrily, declaring: "No one can fairly read the prayers from Greece's town meetings as anything other than explicitly Christian."

Kagan rightly disputed the Kennedy assertions. She pointed out that some of the great Founders--Washington, Jefferson and Madison--took pains to keep sectarian language away from public life.

"The demand for neutrality among religions is not a product of 21st century 'political correctness' but the 18th century view," Kagan said.

During oral argument, she agreed that "language referring repeatedly to Jesus Christ is accepted, admired and important to the majority in the Greece community." But, she added, "it is not accepted by a minority in a public session."

Justices Ginsburg, Breyer and Sotomayor joined the dissent.

Adam Liptak, Supreme Court reporter and analyst, observed: "The perception that partisan politics has infected the court's work may do lasting damage to its prestige, authority and to Americans' faith in the rule of law."

No mays about it. The Roberts Court has no prestige. Its political view of the law destroys any pretense at authority.

As Justin Driver, University of Texas law professor, notes: "it has become increasingly apparent that constitutional law is simply politics by other means."

Meanwhile, the Five Primitives plus one (Justice Breyer) recently upheld a Michigan constitutional amendment that bans affirmative action for admission to state universities--a ruling the New York Times rightly called "blinkered justice."

Again Kennedy, the wood-butcher justice, penned the

obnoxious opinion. He wrote that Michigan voters had exercised their "basic democratic power" in approving the amendment. Voters, like justices, are so often wrong.

Justice Sotomayor disagreed bitterly and passionately in a 58-page dissent joined by Justice Ginsburg. Sotomayor declared that the Constitution required special vigilance in light of "the history of slavery, Jim Crow and recent examples of discriminatory changes to state voting laws."

She ridiculed the Roberts notion that discrimination was "ancient history" and that affirmative action was no longer needed.

Sotomayor cited her own experience: admittance to Princeton and then to Yale law school through affirmative action as a Latina. She had been admitted to the Ivy League "through a special door, living from day-to-day the reality of affirmative action," she pointed out.

She says the Michigan decision puts minorities to a burden not faced by other college applicants: athletes and "legacy" children of alumni. She mocked the unreality of Roberts: born white in the comfortable middle-class of Indiana. (And later a corporate lawyer in Washington who earned $1 million a year.)

In contrast, Sotomayor rose from a housing project in the Bronx. She rightly said at a confirmation hearing "that a wise Latina woman with the richness of her experience would more often than not reach a better conclusion than a white male who hasn't lived that life."

No wonder she is being hailed as "the people's justice," an accolade last bestowed on the great Justice Brandeis.

Sparks Tribune, June 26, 2014

Roberts Court makes law

The five most powerful in America are sitting on the Supreme Court: Chief Justice Roberts and Justices Scalia, Thomas, Alito and Kennedy.

They have more power than presidents and Congress because the justices make law. Chief Justice Roberts claims: "We're not Republicans nor Democrats." He claims that the justices simply call constitutional balls and strikes. Both views are untrue.

The Retrograde Five are highly political and highly partisan despite their judicial robes. Their "fine minds" are pro-corporation and pro-business, anti-people and anti-humane values.

As Roxie Bacon pointed out in the Arizona Attorney magazine review of a book by professor Erwin Chemerinsky:

"With the exception of the Warren Court, the Supreme Court has consistently protected the interests of the wealthy and the powerful even when pitted against such core values as freedom of speech, racial equality, due process and voting rights.

"For most of its history the court failed to perform its one major duty: protecting those who cannot wield sufficient voting power to curtail government abuses against them. Chemerinsky makes his case brilliantly."

The book is "The Case Against the Supreme Court." (Chemerinsky teaches First Amendment law at U.C. Irvine in California.)

Recently the Supreme Court announced it would hear a right-wing challenge to the Affordable Care Act. If the court strikes it down, as is possible, millions of people will lose health coverage under Obamacare.

The court usually grants certiorari when lower circuit courts reach clashing interpretations of the law. Sometimes, however, the court will decide a matter it wasn't asked. Roberts is ruthlessly partisan and political so he easily gets the four votes he needs to hear cases the court should not.

Thom Hartmann in a Truthout op-ed rightly declares that the Roberts Court is turning "America into a constitutional monarchy."

Two cases are illustrative, Citizens United and Shelby County v. Holder.

In Citizens United the court was asked if congressional curbs on political spending applied to pay-per-view movies made by nonprofits. It answered a question it was not asked, ruling that corporations are people and can spend unlimited amounts of money on political campaigns. In astounding judicial overreach, the Reactionary Quintet ruled that under the First Amendment it has free speech protection.

In Holder, the Roberts Court ignored decades of legal precedent to eviscerate the Voting Rights Act. All this suggests that Roberts should be impeached. As William Greider points out in an article in The Nation:

"The GOP majority in control of the court has been legislating on its own, following an agenda aligned with its conservative party. They empowered 'dark money' in politics. They assigned spiritual values to soulless corporations. They blatantly usurp the decision-making that belongs to Congress and the president."

So, yes, he should be impeached. But he won't be. The soon-to-be controlling GOP Senate precludes it.

Sparks Tribune, Dec. 16, 2014

Inside Supreme Court

THE OATH
The Obama White House and the Supreme Court
By Jeffrey Toobin
Doubleday, 298 pages, 2012

This is an important inside look at the Supreme Court but a badly titled book.

The botched oath of office administered by Chief Justice John Roberts to president-elect Barack Obama in 2009 has nothing to do with their sharp disagreement about constitutional interpretation.

Yet author Jeffrey Toobin opens the book with the trivial mistake and goes on and on about a matter of no consequence.

Obama, a constitutional law professor with liberal instincts, was bound to clash with a reactionary chief justice.

In that quarrel, President Obama is right, Roberts wrong. As Toobin puts it: Roberts "has far more often used his formidable skills on behalf of the strong in opposition to the weak." Toobin also rightly said: "The Obama team regards the Supreme Court as just another group of Republicans."

But the chief justice is enormously powerful as shown by his court's retrograde Citizens United ruling of 2010. That decision allowed unlimited campaign funding by declaring money speech protected by the First Amendment.

As wrong as the Roberts decision was, it remains the law of the land. The odds on a constitutional amendment to reverse it are prohibitive.

Toobin is wonderful on Justice Ginzburg, a tiny woman with a huge heart. She disagreed with Justice Blackmun that abortion is a privacy matter.

"Abortion rights are about equality," she said. "The denial of abortion rights to women is just another form of discrimination."

Toobin notes that Ginzburg particularly resented the patronizing of Justice Kennedy in his Carhart abortion decision of 2007, a ruling "straight out of the anti-abortion movement in which he refers to the fetus as a 'baby' and a 'child.'"

It is such "inside stuff" that enhances the Toobin book. Such as: "Liberals want flexible rules that allow courts to reach decisions on the merits and conservatives want strict rules to prevent cases from being heard."

Such as: the court's surprising rule for Obamacare: "Roberts deferred as justices have for 75 years to Congress on issues relating to managing the economy. But it was folly to pretend that Roberts had discovered his inner moderate."

Such as: justices so often try to achieve political results rather than adjudicate cases.

Such as: moderate Republican ideas, like moderate Republicans, have disappeared from the court as they have from the nation.

Such as: Latina Justice Sotomayor proudly declaring: "I am a product of affirmative action."

Such as: Justices Scalia and Breyer are show-offs and Justice Alito writes "clunky sentences" while Justice Breyer opinions ramble.

Toobin sparkles on Justice Souter who declared that the Bush v. Gore decision of 2000 giving the presidency to G.W. Bush "was so political, so transparent that it scarred Souter's belief in the Supreme Court as an institution."

Yet Scalia, confronted by hostile audiences on his frequent speaking tours, could say nothing more intelligent than: "Oh get over it." (That's someone who Toobin describes as an intellectual.)

Souter "came to loathe the Roberts Court," denouncing "its disrespect for precedent, its grasping conservatism and its aggressive pursuit of political objectives."

Toobin is excellent too on Scalia, ridiculing his notions about textualism and originalism, the idea that rights do not exist if they are not stated in the Constitution. Scalia's absurd views ignore the wisdom of Justice Holmes: the law responds to "the felt necessities of the time."

Toobin notes Scalia's hunger to have been named chief justice. He cites Scalia's "belligerence at oral arguments as a way of getting attention--his craving for the spotlight." And declares that Scalia is a conservative "who became a right-wing crank."

That aside, the book is too long by about 100 pages as many books published today are. It's too wordy, desperately needing a stern editor. But Toobin is a star Supreme Court reporter for the New Yorker. Magazine and book editors rarely edit "stars."

Toobin writes about standing--the right to be heard by the Supreme Court--an arcane matter of interest only to lawyers. He writes too much about Justice O'Connor, who had long since left the court. His book is full of clichés, is repetitive and overuses useless "of courses."

Nevertheless, Toobin makes it clear that the Roberts Court is a partisan bunch of Republicans lawmakers harming the nation.

Sparks Tribune, Jan. 10, 2013

Court decries gay couple hatred

The Supreme Court leaped into the 21st century recently by nullifying the 1996 Defense of Marriage Act (DOMA), catching up with public opinion favoring gay marriage.

The court, with the usual 5-4 "political" split, ruled that married same-sex couples are entitled to federal benefits such as health care, Social Security, life insurance and survivor tax policies.

Edith Windsor of New York offers a good example of how survivors in gay marriages will benefit. When her female partner died the IRS refused to treat her as a surviving spouse as it would have for a husband. She was assessed a tax bill of $363,000 for inheritance of her partner's estate.

Justice Kennedy, writing the majority opinion, declared: "DOMA instructed all people with whom same-sex couples interact, including their own children, that their marriage is less worthy than the marriage of others." He said the statute disparaged the dignity of gay couples.

Adam Liptak, Supreme Court reporter for the New York Times, noted that Kennedy announced the opinion to a hushed courtroom "in a stately tone that indicated he was delivering a civil rights landmark."

He was. Justices Breyer, Ginsburg, Kagan and Sotomayor joined his opinion.

Antediluvian sourpuss Justice Scalia complained in his bitter dissent that "anyone opposed to same-sex marriage is an enemy of human decency." He slammed the Kennedy opinion as "a jaw-dropping assertion of judicial supremacy over the will of the people expressed by Congress."

But the determination of the people is often wrong as it was in California's vote to ban gay marriage in Proposition 8.

Other DOMA dissenters were Chief Justice Roberts and Justices Thomas and Alito. Roberts, during oral argument, argued that the institution of marriage "didn't include homosexual couples." He was wrong.

The reality is that gay characters and celebrities are prevalent in America: TV, sports and rap music. Thirty percent of the population lives in states that allow same-sex marriage.

As Martin Luther King said: "The arc of the moral universe is long but it bends toward justice." It did just that in the DOMA ruling.

Affirmative action defeat

The court punted on affirmative action, sending a case originating at the University of Texas, Austin, back to the lower courts for stricter scrutiny.

That means the court, by a 7-1 vote, no longer deems affirmative action necessary. Justice Scalia expressed that view by saying he would overturn any racial preferences.

But Justice Ginsburg in dissent set him and the court straight. She said the plan to take students from the top 10 percent of the state's public high schools was adopted to combat racially segregated schools and neighborhoods.

Ginsburg, a former civil rights lawyer, declared:

"Only an ostrich could regard the supposedly neutral alternatives as race unconscious. State universities need not be blind to the lingering effects of an overtly discriminatory past, the legacy of law-sanctioned inequality.

"Race-consciousness is preferable to some backdoor effort to address inequality by concealing mention of it. Moreover, the University of Texas considers race as but one of many factors in the admissions process."

Justice Ginsburg is so tiny that at oral arguments before the Supreme Court she is barely visible behind the high bench. But her heart and mind are mighty. Amid the dismal Roberts Court, she is stellar.

The Supreme Court almost always rules for the government in national security cases. So it was hardly a surprise that the court recently rejected a challenge to the broadened power of government to eavesdrop on international phone calls and emails.

Writing for the Backward Five in the 5-4 vote, Justice Alito said journalists, lawyers and human rights advocates were unable to show how the congressional law harmed them. He dusted off the ancient court standby: they lacked standing to sue.

Alito, in a circuitous argument, said only the government knows whether the plaintiffs' communications have been intercepted. So he said it was the plaintiffs' burden to prove that they have standing "by pointing to specific facts, not the government's burden to disprove standing by revealing details of its surveillance priorities."

Justice Breyer dissented, joined by the other rational justices, Ginsburg, Kagan and Sotomayor. Breyer declared that the harm done to the plaintiffs was not speculative.

"Indeed, it is as likely to take place as are most future events that common sense inference and ordinary knowledge of human nature tell us will happen," he added.

True. But, alas, the prevailing Supremes are so partisan that common sense means nothing to them.

Sparks Tribune, July 18, 2013

Justices blind on cameras

Members of government institutions sooner or later take on the coloration of that institution.

Take the cases of Justices Sotomayor and Kagan. Both were in favor of camera coverage of Supreme Court oral arguments.

During her confirmation hearings in 2009 Sotomayor was ardently in favor of letting citizens see the Supreme Court at work.

"I have had positive experiences with cameras," she said about serving on U.S. district and circuit courts. "I have happily joined experiments using cameras in my courtroom."

But after four years on the Supreme Court she changed her mind. She now opposes cameras in court. She has become an "upper class snob" just like the other justices who adamantly oppose cameras.

She argues fallaciously that most Americans would not understand Supreme Court arguments and there was no point "in letting them try." Most Americans couldn't care less about the Supreme Court. But for many who do care camera coverage is important.

Adam Liptak, New York Times Supreme Court reporter, labels the Sotomayor comment "an intellectual poll tax that could just as well limit attendance in the courtroom."

Justice Kagan has also done a volte-face. At her confirmation hearings in 2010 she said courtroom cameras "would be a great thing for the institution and, more important, a great thing for the American people."

Now she claims "people might play to the camera" and coverage could be misused. Ridiculous. My experience attending a Supreme Court oral argument revealed extreme respect and even deference to the justices.

The Canadian Supreme Court has televised oral arguments for two decades. Recently that court streamed live on the Internet. Owen Rees, the court's executive director, says "filming has increased the public's access to the court and understanding of its work."

True. But the U.S. Supreme Court insists it is "different." Nonsense. It is unable to give convincing reasons for still veiling the court in the 21st century.

As Kyu Youin, journalism professor and First Amendment scholar at the University of Oregon, remarks: the U.S. Supreme Court betrays "a distinctly American commitment to free expression."

"Many people outside the U.S. are wondering why it is so calcified in its thinking about cameras in the Supreme Court," Youin added.

Answer: because it is also calcified about many of the decisions it hands down.

No consumer recourse

In one of its calcified rulings recently, the court held that consumers seriously harmed by generic drugs don't deserve compensation.

The court, by the usual Retrograde Five margin of 5-4, overturned a lower court decision that awarded $21 million to a woman for pain and suffering caused by reaction to a generic drug. The ruling, which leaves people harmed by generic drugs no recourse, accounts for more than 80 percent of all prescriptions.

As the New York Times editorialized: "It is imperative that the Food and Drug Administration write protective regulations holding generic companies liable for any harm their products cause."

The Times paints a grim picture. The woman, Karen Bartlett of New Hampshire, suffered dreadful injuries after taking a generic version of an anti-inflammatory drug, sulindac, for shoulder pain.

"She developed an extremely severe reaction in which two-thirds of her skin sloughed off," the Times said. "She was left permanently disfigured, legally blind and with permanent damage to her lungs and esophagus."

Justice Alioto, writing for the majority, said the generic company, Mutual Pharmaceutical, was not liable because it had no power to unilaterally change the chemicals or the warning label.

It's a typical made-up reason for a court decision. As the liberal dissenters declared, the company should pay compensation for any harm done and consider taking the drug off the market.

Bar to deportation

In a victory for fairness, the Supreme Court recently ruled, 7-2, that a conviction for marijuana distribution under Georgia law should not result in automatic deportation. A Jamaican, legally in the United States, was ordered deported by an immigration judge.

His offense? Possessing 1.3 grams of pot. The amount makes two cigarettes.

Justice Sotomayor, writing for the majority, noted the absurdity of deportation for a mere misdemeanor.

Wise DNA ruling

The 2012-2013 term just ended produced a wise decision: a ruling that genes are not patentable. It declared unanimously that human DNA isolated from a chromosome cannot be patented because it is a product of nature.

Justice Thomas, in his opinion for the court, declared that granting patents on natural phenomena would inhibit innovation, "at odds with the very point of patents: promotion of creation."

Sparks Tribune, July 25, 2013

Money despoils democracy

In Citizens United (2010) the Supreme Court reaffirmed earlier declarations that money is speech. Democracy had already been corrupted with legalized bribery in the form of campaign contributions.

After Citizens United the New York Times exploded:

"The Supreme Court has thrust politics back to the Robber Baron era of the 19th century. Disingenuously waving the flag of the First Amendment, the court's majority has paved the way for corporations to use their vast treasuries to win elections."

The late historian Howard Zinn put the matter in perspective:

"No one can stop us from getting on a soapbox and speaking. We might reach 100 people that way. But if we were Proctor and Gamble, which makes the soapbox, we could buy prime time for TV commercials and buy full-page ads in newspapers, reaching several million. How much freedom we have depends on how much money we have."

Two conservative nonprofits, Crossroads Grassroots Policy Strategies and Americans for Prosperity, have already poured $60 million into TV ads to influence the 2012 presidential outcome.

The $60 million dwarfs the amount spent by all super PACs put together. Nonprofits don't have to disclose their sources. Super PACs do.

The dark hand of GOP Svengali Karl Rove is pushing Crossroads. Americans for Prosperity is funded by the billionaires David and Charles Koch.

A new book by Christopher Hayes, "Twilight of the Elites," is even more disturbing.

"While the logic of democracy is one person, one vote,

our entire system of representation heavily favors those with the money," Hayes writes.

Money grants access to the powerful. Money pays for lobbyists, PACs and hefty political donations.

Money enables the hiring of power attorneys who manipulate the tax code to allow "oligarchs to keep scores of billions from the IRS."

Politicians, too, are in cahoots with the One Percenters. The Bush tax cuts granted the rich $82 billion. President Obama, alas, extended them.

Citizens United is just one of many horrible rulings by the Supreme Court. In Plessy v. Ferguson (1896) the court upheld Southern apartheid.

In Santa Clara County v. Southern Pacific Railroad (1886), the headnote to the official report, written by the court reporter, declared that corporations were people and entitled to constitutional rights. The justices did not say that.

In another reactionary decision, Lochner v. New York (1905), the court reversed a legislative limit of a 10-hour day and 60-hour week for bakers.

Justice Rufus Peckham, writing for a 5-4 majority, outrageously declared that such statutes "limiting the hours in which grown and intelligent men may labor to earn their living are mere meddlesome interference with the rights of the individual."

Justice Harlan I dissented, rightly complaining that employer and employee are not on equal footing. Bosses have the upper hand. Always have. Always will.

In 1895 the Supreme Court voided a congressional income tax law. The vote was 5-4 with five wealthy justices killing it.

The court in Schenck (1919) ruled that harmless leaflets were a "clear and present danger" to national security under the 1917 Espionage Act.

The absurdity was manifest. Yet ever since the court has nearly always taken the side of purported national security.

In Adkins v. Children's Hospital (1923), the court invalidated a minimum wage for women workers in the District of Columbia. Justice George Sutherland said it was "simply and exclusively a price-fixing law."

In dissent, Chief Justice William Taft pointed out that employees "are particularly subject to the overreaching of the harsh and greedy employer."

In another terrible ruling, the Supreme Court in 2000 upheld the right of Big Tobacco to advertise cigarettes, a product that kills 500,000 Americans yearly. Corporate freedom and the merchants of death prevailed over the health of Americans.

The historic pro-business bias of the court is obvious. From 1880 to 1937, historian Henry Steele Commager noted, "the political field was strewn with the corpses of social welfare laws struck down by judicial weapons." In the early 1930s the court repealed the progressive New Deal.

Justice Samuel Miller, Iowan who served on the court from 1862 to 1890, summed up reality:

"It is vain to contend with judges who have been, at the bar, the advocates of railroad companies and all the forms of associated capital when they are called on to decide cases. All their training, all their feelings, are in favor of those who need no such influence."

And that is precisely why Earl Warren was the greatest chief justice. He put people over property, human needs over the money-making demands of capitalism.

Sparks Tribune, Aug. 19, 2012

Court clings to woeful ruling

Republicans rule the retrograde House because of the misguided voting of the American people, the Senate because of the unconstitutional filibuster and the Supreme Court because of reactionary political decisions.

Democracy is a huge loser in all three cases.

The disastrous Supreme Court decision of Citizens United in 2010, equating money with speech, gave the superrich a far greater First Amendment than nearly all Americans have.

What the decision means was illustrated just the other day: the Koch brothers and their fellow money barons will spend $400 million in private money to defeat President Obama this fall.

The amount, unprecedented in American political history, is no one's idea of democracy except for the five-man majority of the Supreme Court.

Given an opportunity to reverse Citizens United the court again repudiated democracy.

The court Monday summarily struck down a decision by the Montana Supreme Court that had upheld a state law limiting political spending by corporations.

The opinion was unsigned by the Gutless Five: Chief Justice Roberts and Justices Scalia, Thomas, Kennedy and Alito.

The court did not have the courtesy and judicial wisdom to hold oral arguments and let briefs be submitted. Such legal necessities could have shown just how outrageous Citizens United is.

It is arbitrary and impertinent to decide a case without adequate information and deliberation. Sadly, such a tactic is typical of the Republican court presided over by Roberts.

No means no, the court said in effect. It said Citizens United clearly "applies to the Montana state law."

But in dissent for the liberal bloc of four, Justice Stephen Breyer declared that Citizens United was a mistake, that it was wrong for the court to have assumed "independent expenditures do not corrupt."

"Given the history and political landscape in Montana, the state court had a compelling interest in limiting expenditures by corporations," Breyer declared.

Mike McGrath, chief justice of the Montana court, stressed in his opinion that state politics had been corrupted by corporate interests so the law was justified.

"Montana had been operating under a mere shell of legal authority and the real social and political power was wielded by powerful corporate managers to further their own business interests," McGrath wrote.

The state's "copper kings," who controlled a huge chunk of the state's wealth, blatantly bribed legislators.

A New York Times editorial summed up the Supreme Court ruling: the retrograde majority "turned itself into a copper kings' court."

Foes of Citizens United and some legal authorities urge a constitutional amendment to foil a clearly partisan court. But the math of that is prohibitive. It explains why a constitutional amendment to reverse Citizens United is most unlikely.

A constitutional amendment requires a super majority of two-thirds vote in each house of Congress before approval of the states is sought. A high hurdle indeed!

But an even higher hurdle: three-fourths of the states must ratify the proposed amendment. That means 38 states, an awesome number.

(The Constitution can be changed by constitutional convention but precious few want to take that route. A convention would pose a dire threat to American civil liberties embodied by the Constitution's Bill of Rights.)

As for Montana, it has one of the most transparent democracies in the world.

Its governor, Brian Schweitzer, has an open-door policy for all Montanans. As he says, "I'm just a rancher"-- like many others in the state.

In an op-edit column in the Times, Schweitzer eloquently told why Montana insisted on keeping corporate money out of politics.

"A miner named William Clark came upon a massive copper vein near Butte," he wrote. "It was the largest deposit on earth. Overnight he became one of the wealthiest men in the world.

"He bought up half the state of Montana. If he needed favors from politicians he bought those as well.

"In 1899 he wanted to become a U.S. senator. (State legislatures then appointed U.S. senators.) Clark simply gave each corruptible lawmaker $10,000."

So Clark became a U.S. senator. But the Senate soon kicked him out when it learned of the bribes. This caused the bought-and-paid-for senator to rightfully complain that he "never bought a man who wasn't for sale."

Schweitzer concluded that the Clark case prompted Montana citizens to approve a ballot initiative banning corporate money from campaigns.

Today large campaign contributions are legalized bribery, a political corruption twice sanctioned by the Supreme Court.

No wonder so many American citizens have lost faith in this so-called democracy.

Sparks Tribune, July 1, 2012

Court upholds right to lie

The 2011-2012 term of the Supreme Court, now close to becoming "ancient history," was mixed. It justly upheld the Obamacare health plan but reiterated its woeful stance in Citizens United that money is speech.

Aside from the Citizen United ruling favorable to the One Percenters, the court is good on most First Amendment issues.

In the last term it extended constitutional protection to the right to lie.

The case arose after Congress enacted the Stolen Valor Act in 2006. The act made it a crime for someone to falsely claim he was a Medal of Honor winner.

The claim by Xavier Alvarez, an ex-Marine, was an utter fabrication. But as reprehensible as the lie was, the court rightly ruled that the First Amendment barred criminalizing speech.

It upheld the 9th U.S. Circuit Court of Appeals ruling that if the act were allowed to stand it would leave "wide areas of public discourse to the mercies of the truth police."

The court also wisely held that mandatory lifetime sentences for juveniles convicted of murder--without hope of parole--was cruel and unusual punishment barred by the Eighth Amendment.

Justice Kagan, writing for the majority, said the Constitution forbids "requiring all youth convicted of homicide to receive lifetime incarceration regardless of their age and the nature of their crimes."

She cited the gross injustice of a lifetime sentence for a 14-year-old boy who was merely standing by while someone else killed a store clerk.

"This mandatory punishment disregards the possibility of rehabilitation even when the circumstances most suggest it," Kagan said.

Her opinion was a sterling answer to reactionary Justice Scalia who sneered during oral argument: "I thought that modern penology has abandoned that rehabilitation thing."

In another June ruling, the court unfortunately sustained the centerpiece of the vicious Arizona 2010 anti-immigration law, "the show-me-your-papers" provision.

The ACLU released emails showing that the law was racially motivated against Latinos.

But on a positive note, the court ruled that immigration law is the prerogative of Congress and the president. It declared that states cannot adopt laws or enforcement policies that conflict with federal law. They cannot make "foreign policy."

As the New York Times wrote in an editorial: "This should be the final warning to Arizona and copycat states like Alabama: stop concocting criminal dragnets for civil violators."

Nevertheless, the nation is still far short of the DREAM Act proposed by President Obama.

Namely: a halt to deportation of undocumented immigrants who came to America as children. They must be under 30 and have come when they were under 16.

Furthermore, they must have lived in this country for five years, be an honorably discharged veteran or a high school graduate and not convicted of a felony.

On another upbeat note, the Supreme Court ruled in favor of CBS which had been fined an absurd amount--$550,000--by the FCC for showing a nano-second of Janet Jackson's breast during a Super Bowl broadcast in 2004.

In a companion case, the court backed two other broadcasters, Fox Television and ABC. The FCC had declared that they violated what it prudishly called indecency standards: a fleeting expletive on Fox and seven seconds of a woman's bare rear end on ABC.

Fox in 2002 aired Cher, receiving a Billboard Music

Award, saying that critics for 40 years have been calling her "washed up." "Yeah, right," she said. "Fuck 'em." The ABC broadcast was a 2003 "NYPD Blue" episode.

(Cable stations have no restrictions on so-called obscenity because their programs are not regulated by the FCC.)

The Supreme Court, however, remains mired in squeamishness. In the court's ruling on the Fox and ABC cases, the opinion by Justice Kennedy referred to the "F-word."

The word is commonplace everywhere except in the puritanical precincts of the Supreme Court.

The Roberts Court also showed its hostility to organized labor by upholding, in effect, right-to-work laws in 23 states. In the Knox decision it said unions cannot spend dues for political causes.

Corporations have no such restrictions.

"The Supreme Court's ruling in Knox v. Service Employees International Union is one of the most brazen of the Roberts Court," a Times editorial declared.

In dissent, Justice Sotomayor deplored the court's violation of its own rules and disregard of "principles of judicial restraint that define the court's proper role in the American system of separated powers."

This hatred of labor is indicative of the Roberts Court's general thrust: a Republican politics ignoring so much grim reality in American society.

Sparks Tribune, Aug. 5, 2012

Obamacare OK'd but inadequate

President Roosevelt, frustrated because New Deal legislation enacted by Congress was constantly being struck down by a reactionary Supreme Court, announced a plan to expand the court from nine to 15 members so he could pick his kind of justices.

Suddenly, Justice Owen Roberts changed course to uphold New Deal measures. This prompted wags to quip: "A switch in time saves nine."

Chief Justice John Roberts (no relation to Justice Roberts) was under no threat of a court-packing plan by President Obama. But he just as suddenly switched from his usual retrograde stance to join the court's four liberals to declare Obamacare constitutional.

The reversal recently by the leader of the corporate-loving Supreme Court was as astonishing as it was welcome.

Roberts joined Justices Ginsburg, Breyer, Kagan and Sotomayor to uphold the Patient Protection and Affordable Care Act.

Why did a Republican politician like Roberts suddenly act like a justice instead of a CEO?

An educated guess is that he felt it was time to act like a statesman if he wanted to restore some of the court's reputation tarnished under his stewardship.

Adam Liptak, New York Times Supreme Court reporter, phrased it this way: he sought to return "credibility, prestige, authority and legitimacy" to the court.

Even corporations need some good will.

The health care ruling was one of the rare times Roberts took the liberal side in more than one hundred 5-4 rulings.

Certainly 50 million uninsured Americans were grateful for the switch. And so were:

• 2.5 million who can be kept on their parents' insurance plans up to the age of 26.

• 18 million children with pre-existing health conditions who cannot be denied insurance.

• Insurance companies do not have unchecked power to cancel policies, deny coverage or charge women more than men.

• Preventive care like mammograms for women and wellness visits for seniors are covered free by insurance companies.

Columnist Paul Krugman observed that Obamacare makes America a little kinder and a little more decent.

Roberts in his opinion said the requirement that most Americans buy health insurance or pay a penalty falls under the power of Congress to tax for the "general welfare."

But one downside of the Roberts ruling is that Medicaid coverage will be left to the pinch-penny mercies of retrograde states like Texas. The opinion allows states to reject Medicaid.

Roberts wrongly called such a provision "economic dragooning."

But as a matter of fact, as one critic noted, the law allows states "to dragoon" federal funds without providing coverage for which those funds are intended.

In a stinging dissent, Justice Kennedy called "the entire act before us is invalid in its entirety."

Indeed, that was the view many expected Roberts to take after seeming to accept the silly "broccoli argument" during oral discussion (government could force Americans to buy broccoli).

Nevertheless, widespread Democratic rejoicing over the decision is unwarranted.

The nation is still without universal health coverage, a program FDR was urging eight decades ago. Most Democratic presidents ever since at least feinted at national health. Even Republican President Nixon supported it.

Americans often revile "communist Cuba." Yet those "dreaded" communists have universal health care, free college education, free day care and 12-week paid maternity leave.

That's humane socialism as opposed to heartless capitalism.

Obama, as is his wont, refused to fight for truly progressive single-payer legislation, yielding to the insurance companies and Big Pharma.

Columnist Robert Scheer pointed out: "Obama limited his ambition to what Big Pharma and the insurance giants would accept as 'reform' in a system that they had so successfully exploited. Obamacare is a faux reform."

Many poor people remain uninsured. Medical costs are steadily rising. The only solution is universal health care paid for by taxpayers.

The World Health Organization lists America as a pitiful 37th in the world in health care even though it is the richest nation. Moreover, America has the most costly health care in the world.

The great Justice Brandeis spoke of how "a single courageous state may serve as a laboratory" for the nation. That single courageous state is Vermont.

A year ago its legislature enacted universal health care, the first and only state to do so.

A federal national health plan is not a privilege. It is a basic human right, an ethical right that all nations should have.

Sparks Tribune, July 15, 2012

Pain of free speech

Free speech is often painful but it is the price we pay for having the First Amendment, the greatest glory of America.

Americans are appalled by protests at military funerals. How could anyone be so despicable, so callous at such a sorrowful occasion?

Whatever your answer the fact is that obnoxious protesters are protected by the First Amendment.

Chief Justice Roberts, writing for the Supreme Court majority in the case of protests at military funerals, said the national commitment to free speech is paramount. That commitment requires protection of "even hurtful speech on public issues to ensure that we do not stifle public debate."

Roberts quoted from the landmark Sullivan libel decision of 1964: "Debate on public issues should be robust, uninhibited and wide-open." Speech on public issues "occupies the highest rung of the hierarchy of First Amendment values," he continued.

"Speech is powerful. It can stir people to action, move them to tears of both joy and sorrow and--as it did here-- inflict great pain."

The "here" referred to protests at the funeral of Marine Lance Cpl. Matthew Snyder who was killed in Iraq. His father, Albert Snyder, sued the protesters for inflicting emotional distress.

The protesters were six members of the Westboro Baptist Church of Topeka, Kan. They appeared at the funeral in Westminster, Md., carrying signs that read "God hates fags" and "Fags doom nations."

The church, founded by the Rev. Fred Phelps, contends that God is punishing America because it tolerates homosexuality.

A jury in the U.S. district court of Maryland found for Snyder. But the 4th U.S. Circuit Court of Appeals reversed on First Amendment grounds. That decision was upheld by the Supreme Court.

The dissenter in the 8-1 decision, Justice Alito, cited the "fighting words" doctrine of the Chaplinsky decision of 1942. That decision, of dubious constitutionality today, held that such words do not have First Amendment protection.

"Our profound national commitment to free and open debate is not a license for vicious verbal assault," Alito wrote. "It is not necessary to allow the brutalization of innocent victims."

Alito echoes what so many Americans think. Nevertheless, Roberts was right. "We cannot react to that pain by punishing the speaker," he said.

The Supreme Court, so often a reactionary, corporate-loving body, has been particularly vigilant about protecting the First Amendment.

Last year it ruled that crush videos, as abhorrent as they are, deserve First Amendment protection. Such videos depict women crushing small animals with spiked high heels as a sexual fetish.

Once again Alito was the sole dissenter, arguing that the harm animals suffer in dog fights is enough to sustain a 1999 law of Congress limiting Internet sales of crush videos.

But Alito should ponder the words of Justice Felix Frankfurter in the 1950 case of Rabinowitz v. the United States: "It is a fair summary of history to say that the safeguards of liberty have often been forged in controversies involving not very nice people."

Funeral protesters are nauseous people. So are devotees of crush videos. But even nauseous people deserve First Amendment protection.

DNA suits OK'd

The Supreme Court earlier this month eased the way for inmates to sue to get DNA evidence that might prove their innocence. It ruled that a death row prisoner in Texas could sue a prosecutor under a federal civil rights law for access to that information.

Archreactionary Justice Thomas complained in dissent that the courts would be flooded with civil rights suits. But Justice Ginsburg, who wrote the majority opinion, responded with wit: the decision was unlikely to prompt "any litigation flood--or even rainfall."

Sparks Tribune, March 20, 2011

Executing Insane Wrong

The death penalty is clearly a violation of the Eighth Amendment bar to "cruel and unusual punishment." But the Constitution means nothing in the state of Texas, the murder capital of the world.

Texas planned to execute Scott Panetti on Dec. 3 although he is criminally insane. But the 5th circuit appeals court in New Orleans stayed the execution. Panetti, convicted of murdering his in-laws with a hunting rifle in 1995, has a 30-year record of severe mental illness.

Representing himself, Panetti turned his trial into a tragicomedy. He wore a cowboy suit. He wanted to subpoena Jesus Christ and John F. Kennedy. He was suffering such delusions that he said Satan was directing his trial and execution.

Panetti was discharged from the Navy at 18. Eighteen months later he was diagnosed with "early schizophrenia." After that he was hospitalized several times for delusions and psychotic episodes.

The Supreme Court in 1986 declared that executing the insane would serve no purpose and be "savage and inhumane." It certainly would. But the savagery and inhumanity of the death penalty will continue until the distant day when the Supreme Court rules it unconstitutional.

Sparks Tribune, Dec. 9, 2014

GOP pols rule Supremes

WASHINGTON--The reverential tone prevailing here at the Supreme Court is unjustified by its many horrible decisions for more than a century.

The Dred Scott ruling in 1857 said Negroes could never be citizens, that they were "beings of an inferior order" and that they "had no rights which the white man was bound to respect."

In 1886 in Southern Pacific Railroad the court declared that corporations were people and hence entitled to constitutional rights.

In 2000 in Bush v. Gore the court made a Republican president even though the Democrat had 550,000 more popular votes. In 2010 in Citizens United the court granted corporations First Amendment rights, upholding previous rulings that money is speech.

And just last month the Corporate Court ruled in AT&T Mobility that consumers cannot band together in class-action suits to pursue justifiable complaints--a crushing blow to consumer rights.

The last three cases were decided 5-4 by five Republican politicians.

Yet the portrait gallery here cheered me.

Louis Brandeis was the greatest of the 112 justices and chief justices who have served on the court since 1790. Brandeis, the people's lawyer who became the people's justice, served from 1916 to 1939. The portrait here shows him both benign and serious.

Two of my favorite justices are Hugo Black (1937-1971) and Bill Douglas (1939-1975). They were superb on the First Amendment. The luminescent portrait of Black was painted from a photo by Yousuf Karsch, great photographer who took the "bulldog" portrait of Churchill.

Pictured also is Earl Warren, greatest chief justice. He ruled for people as opposed to Chief Justice John Marshall who ruled for property.

Real cool

As young people say these days, it was cool to be in the Supreme Court inner sanctum to hear oral argument in the case of Nevada Ethics Commission v. Carrigan (Sparks city councilman).

I observed and heard the justices for the first time after years of teaching and writing about them and the court. The questioning by the justices was lively with counsel for both sides bombarded by tough queries.

The courtroom is awesome: four white marble columns on four sides with ionic capitals and a 44-foot-high rosette ceiling. The justices appear from behind a curtain like nine popes.

New York Times accounts of oral argument usually suggest how the justices will rule. But in the Carrigan case the result is uncertain.

A guess: the court will find for the commission because ethics trumps the law and Carrigan's First Amendment argument is far-fetched.

Sparks Tribune, May 15, 2011

Partisan reality of top court

THE NINE. Inside the Secret World of the Supreme Court
By Jeffrey Toobin
411 pp., Anchor Paperback, 2008.

Supreme Court nomination hearings have become a game of charades. The senators preen and pontificate and the nominees are evasive and disingenuous.

When nominee Sonia Sotomayor was grilled recently, a senator asked: "Can you be objective?"

Sure, she said, in an appeasing way. But she should have replied: "As objective as Chief Justice Roberts and Justices Scalia, Kennedy, Thomas and Alito."

Such an answer, while true, would not have been politic. But the Reactionary Five is hardly objective. It is as partisan as any politician.

Roberts, in his nomination hearing, said "judges are not politicians" but simply umpires.

Malarkey.

Judge Learned Hand, one of America's best jurists who never served on the Supreme Court, observed: "It is the way of judges to disguise what they are doing and impute to it a derivative far more imperative than their personal preferences, which are all that lie behind their decisions."

And Chief Justice Hughes told a young Justice Douglas when he joined the court: "At the constitutional level where we work, ninety percent of any decision is emotional. The rationale part of us supplies the reasons for supporting our predilections."

After the egregious Bush v. Gore decision in 2000, former Justice Souter called the majority opinion what it was: crudely partisan.

The Toobin look, an inside look at the Supreme Court, tells similar truths as "The Brethren" did. Written by Bob Woodward and Scott Armstrong 20 years ago, "The Brethren" described Chief Justice Burger as the "pompous, egomaniacal and bumbler" he was.

Toobin's frankness is in the same vein. He writes:

• Former Justice O'Connor, no radical, called G.W. Bush "arrogant, lawless, incompetent and extreme."

• Justice Kennedy has "a weakness for high-flown, sometimes meaningless rhetoric."

• Justice Stevens is "dignified, clear-headed...his eloquence honors the court."

• Justice Scalia displays juvenile impetulance, calling people idiots when they disagree with his originalist view of the Constitution.

• Justice Thomas, a "white black," is so retrograde that just one of his first 40 clerks was black.

Sparks Tribune, Jan. 10, 2010

Carrigan wrong, wrong

Mike Carrigan is a good guy, an honest guy. But he is also a stubborn guy.

Even after the U.S. Supreme Court ruled unanimously against him on an ethical position he remained defiant. He thinks he's right, the court is wrong and so are nationwide ethical codes.

He still insists that the Nevada ethics law is "unconstitutionally vague" as to what is an ethical conflict.

Maybe. But maybe it's also a case of a former Navy careerist with a military mind-set refusing to take no for an answer.

Carrigan, Sparks councilman, is also wrong in refusing to talk with reporters from the Sparks Tribune.

He says some of the Trib coverage of him has been biased and unfair. Possibly. But unless newspapers praise politicians, their coverage is considered distorted, one-sided and slanted.

As always, it takes two to quarrel. This columnist does not know who or what started the feud. But he does know that it is wrong for Carrigan to maintain a childish snit.

Public officials must talk to the press whether they like to or not. It is essential that they give the readers their side of any issue.

It is also essential that the press maintain its watchdog role, "to bark" at anything suspicious.

And it is essential for public officials to understand that the voters are their bosses and that the press represents the readers, not the politicians.

The pols don't have all the answers any more than the press does. But the dialogue must be open between the governed and governors. It serves no purpose to use "bad coverage" as an excuse to remain silent.

Councilman Carrigan and Nathan Orme, editor of this newspaper, need to bury whatever are their "ancient animosities." Not for Carrigan's sake or for the Tribune's sake. But for the sake of Trib readers.

As for the recent Supreme Court decision, it was a blow to the Carrigan ego. The prevailing 5-4 court majority is reactionary Republican. Carrigan is no reactionary but he is a Republican.

The court is seldom unanimous about anything but it voted 9-0 against him.

Unlike a decision in an admiralty case that nobody cares about, a Supreme Court ruling on ethics is important to politicians--and above all to the people.

The U.S. Supreme Court emphatically rejected the Carrigan viewpoint. It reversed the Nevada Supreme Court which had toppled a censorious decision by the Nevada Ethics Commission. And it ruled that ethical laws for legislators are as old as the union.

Jefferson, presiding over the Senate in the early days of the Republic, adopted a recusal policy for the sake of decency and for "the fundamental principles of the social compact which denies to any man to be a judge in his own case."

Justice Scalia, writing the court's opinion, noted: "Virtually every state has enacted some type of recusal law, many of which, not unlike Nevada's, require public officials to abstain from voting on all matters presenting a conflict of interest."

Carrigan voted for a casino backed by his friend and campaign manager--a clear conflict of interest. That fact hardly makes him dishonest. But the principle is everything.

Scalia is as right as rain in the Carrigan ruling. But the irony is obvious when it comes to *his* ethics.

Scalia participated in the case of former Vice President Dick Cheney's failure to disclose records of his secret energy task force. Scalia should have recused himself because he went duck hunting with his pal Cheney and rode the vice presidential plane to Louisiana for the hunt.

Scalia scoffed at the notion that he could be bought so cheaply--which is beside the point. (The reactionary Cheney did not have to buy the vote of the reactionary Scalia.)

Most recently Scalia was asked to recuse himself from a Walmart sex discrimination suit because his son is co-chairman of labor and employment practice at the law firm representing Walmart.

Not only did Scalia refuse, he provided the fifth vote Monday in yet another outrageous pro-business decision by the Partisan Five. Scalia should also "cast out the beam" in his own eye along with that in Carrigan's.

Justice Thomas, who has many ethical problems of his own, at least had the decency to recuse himself from a VMI case because his son went to school there.

Politicians throughout the nation, including the five Supreme Court politicians, must be like Caesar's wife: above suspicion.

Sparks Tribune, June 26, 2011

More Woeful Decisions

Court belittles sex bias case

What the Supreme Court badly needs is two more women. A majority of five women would give the court the empathy it woefully lacks.

The court is now ruled by five archconservatives, four of them white and fossilized. The fifth reactionary is black but even "whiter" and crustier than the other four.

Supreme Court oral argument recently on the sex discrimination suit against Walmart proves the point.

• Walmart has greatly underpaid women in the same jobs and with the same titles as men.

• Walmart has a terrible record of promoting men rather than women even though the women are often far more qualified.

Yes, sadly, it is still a man's world.

The sex-bias case arose in 1999 when Stephanie Odle was fired because she complained about sex discrimination.

And, boy, did she have a doozy of a complaint. As an assistant manager of a Walmart store she discovered that a man with the same title and far less experience was making $10,000 a year more than she was.

The three woman on the court--Justices Ginsburg, Sotomayor and Kazan--during oral argument honed in on gender bias in the work place.

"It isn't at all complicated," Ginsburg said. "A decision maker...would prefer someone who looked like him."

Kagan observed that Walmart's practice may violate civil rights laws.

But two of the "old men," Justices Scalia and Kennedy, made it clear that a court majority would reject the class-action suit as far too broad, involving 1.5 million past and present women employees.

Moreover, Kennedy asked: "What's the unlawful policy that Walmart has adopted?" After all, he insisted, the company has a written policy calling for equal treatment without regard to sex.

Surely a Supreme Court justice should know the difference between calling for something and doing something.

A lawyer for the women rightly argued that the corporate culture is all-pervasive, teaching the mostly male supervisors that women are less aggressive than men and therefore less suited to being managers.

Another fact is plain: when the suit was filed against the nation's largest retailer, two-thirds of its employees were women but 86 percent of the store managers were men.

A federal trial court judge rightly ruled for the women. So did the 9th U.S. Court of Appeals, the best court in America. But Supreme Court reactionaries decide the law of the land. Their rulings are seldom good.

Predictions are risky in the newspaper business. Nevertheless, it is apparent from questioning by the justices that Walmart women will lose.

The slogan carved on the façade of the Supreme Court building, "Equal Justice Under Law," is false. Women do not get equal justice.

Court denies justice

The just cause lost.

Cardinal Newman of England ("Apologia pro Vita Sua") in a letter to a friend in 1843.

Justice Thomas has long been a disgrace to the Supreme Court. But he outdid himself in outrageousness in a decision he recently authored for the retrograde camp.

The case, Connick v. Thompson, dealt with the wrongful conviction of John Thompson because New Orleans prosecutors withheld evidence that would have cleared him of a murder charge.

He spent 18 years in prison, 14 on Death Row. He was exonerated when a prosecutor confessed. A trial court found for Thompson, awarding him $14 million damages for wrongful imprisonment.

But predictably the Robert Court overturned the judgment, 5-4. Thomas wrote that the prosecutor's office could not be held liable for a single incident of wrong-doing.

Spoken like a right-wing ideologue for a supposedly nonpolitical body.

Dahlia Lithwick of Slate magazine called it "one of the meanest Supreme Court decisions ever."

It was. Thomas is the so-called justice who wrote that a prisoner had no constitutional claim even though he was slammed to a concrete floor, punched and kicked by a guard after he asked for a grievance form.

Justice Scalia wrote a concurring opinion in that barbarous decision. Scalia is the so-called justice who wrote in 2009 that the Constitution does not forbid "the execution of a convicted defendant who had a full and fair trial but is later able to convince a habeas court that he is 'actually' innocent."

Conservatives often say the Supreme Court is on the side of criminals. No, they are usually on the side of due process: fairness, decent treatment and opposition to tyrannical use of power.

Thomas and Scalia oppose the very spirit of due process. Montesquieu expressed the humanist point of view in "The Spirit of Laws," declaring justice to be the supreme virtue of government.

Sparks Tribune, April 10, 2011

Court denounced--again

It is the way of judges to disguise what they are doing and impute to it a derivative far more imperative than their personal preferences--which are all that lie behind their decisions.
Judge Learned Hand

The term just ended may have been the worst in the 223-year history of the Supreme Court.

If that seems like a gross exaggeration consider:

• The court rejected a huge class-action suit against discriminatory Walmart.

• It shielded the makers of generic drugs from lawsuits by patients who had been harmed.

• It smothered lawsuits against mutual fund liars and cheaters.

• It disallowed suits over religious funding, pollution and failure to turn over exculpating evidence for a death row inmate.

• It struck down an exemplary Arizona campaign-funding statute.

Its pro-business bias was so blatant that the court earned the nickname of Corporative Court. The votes were almost always 5-4 along the repulsive ideological divide.

The reason for the miscarriages of justice is simple: the justices are politicians not judges.

A headline in The New York Review summed up the October-to-June term perfectly: "The court's embarrassingly bad decisions."

Beneath the headline is an excoriating article written by Ronald Dworkin.

The court is dominated by five right-wingers who "continue to revise our historical Constitution" and offer arguments "of poor quality," Dworkin writes.

The five are interpreting "the abstract clauses of the Constitution to match their own political convictions" and inventing "arguments that disguise rather than exhibit actual motivating opinions."

Above all, Dworkin notes: "In the last few years they have overruled a series of important precedents and reversed several long-standing constitutional traditions.

"They have flatly prohibited sensible race-conscious social and educational policies, bolstered government's support for religion and progressively narrowed the scope of abortion rights.

"They have changed the American electoral system to make the election of Republican candidates more likely by guaranteeing corporations a constitutional right to spend as much as they wish."

Despite this blistering indictment, Adam Liptak, Supreme Court reporter for the New York Times, says the term "was marked by accomplishment." It's hard to see where.

The court was laudably steadfast on the First Amendment. It ruled for the Mighty First on rebarbative funeral protesters, sickening crush videos and disgusting video games.

It rightly declared the overcrowding of California prisons cruel and unusual punishment.

Justice Kennedy, writing for the court, said the system failed to deliver adequate medical and mental health care and produced "needless suffering and death." Kennedy added: suicidal inmates were jammed into "telephone booth-sized cages without toilets."

But little else was praiseworthy. So-called national security covers a multitude of sins, including torture. The court declined to review the case of five individuals who were kidnapped and tortured in prisons overseas.

A New York Times editorial rightly called the inaction "a major stain on American justice."

"By slamming the door on these victims without explanation it removed the essential judicial block against the executive branch's use of claims of secrecy to cover up misconduct that shocks the conscience," the Times said.

In another dreadful decision, the Supreme Court made it still harder for whistle-blowers to hold government contractors accountable for fraud.

The False Claims Act seeks to encourage whistle-blowers. The court ruling does just the opposite. As the Times noted: "Justice Thomas' opinion is wrong about the text, context and history of the law."

The court again breached the wall separating church and state, upholding a $350 million disbursement by Arizona to religious schools. Justice Kagan rightly savaged the majority for "ravaging one of this nation's defining constitutional commitments."

Kagan also correctly dissented when the court killed Arizona's public matching funds in political campaigns. She said the law "subsidizes and produces more political speech" rather than the court's crabbed view that it restricts speech.

But the dissenters don't make the law. What prevails is Justice Alito's weep-for-the-wealthy view that the statute diminished "the effectiveness of the rich candidate's spending."

Things will get worse before they get better. The forecast is for the court to move even farther to the Right next term--if that is possible. Unfortunately the nation is stuck with the Horrible Five.

But at least their names should be etched in ignominy: Chief Justice Roberts and Justices Scalia, Thomas, Alito and Kennedy.

Scalia, the Tea Party justice, is the worst. He has said egregiously: "Mere factual innocence is no reason not to carry out a death sentence properly reached."

Yet that so-called justice is helping to make the law of the land.

Sparks Tribune, July 10, 2011

Roberts Court: Retrograde 5

President Bush mercifully has left the White House but his Supreme Court legacy will plague the nation for decades.

The court is a corporate and business body doing the bidding of the Republican Party.

Proof: the court took the side of the U.S. Chamber of Commerce in 13 of 16 cases during the 2009-2010 term.

It was ever thus as a new book by Jeff Shesol makes clear. Shesol's "Supreme Power" details Franklin Roosevelt's clash with court reactionaries because of its systematic destruction of the New Deal.

As Walter Lippmann, highly respected columnist of the era, put it: the Hughes Court of the 1930s was "out of harmony with the needs" of the vast majority of people.

Then, as now, a constant stream of 5-4 decisions kept the nation benighted despite the overwhelming mandate for FDR during the Great Depression. After the 1934 mid-term election Roosevelt Democrats controlled both the House and Senate by crushing 75 percent margins.

Yet then, as now, the court is considered by many people a "sacred shrine," "a secular priesthood." The justices were and are "black-robed gods." They were and are pure: without politics and prejudices.

The truth is otherwise. The names of the "players" change but court politicking continues despite the holy guise.

The most outrageous of the many outrageous decisions by the Roberts Court this term was Citizens United. It declared that corporate money is speech. The First Amendment may be America's greatest glory but it was never intended for faceless corporations.

Not satisfied with having established their Republican bona fides, the court struck down an Arizona law that tried to level the political playing field. The court nullified a statute giving matching funds to candidates running against privately funded opponents.

In still another egregious ruling, the court voided all state and local gun control laws. It used the musty old argument that the Second Amendment prohibits such laws.

Never mind, as Justice Breyer noted in dissent, that handguns yearly cause 10,000 deaths and 40,000 injuries. The Chicago ordinance that was shot down was an effort to curb school gunplay. Thirty-two school kids were killed in Chicago last year and 226 injured.

Many states and cities imposed curbs to alleviate such carnage. Now the nefarious National Rifle Association is still freer to promote mayhem.

So-called national security nearly always trumps the First Amendment. So it was business as usual for the Roberts Court when it ruled that legal and political training offered by the Humanitarian Law Project was abetting terrorists.

In dissent Justice Breyer had it right: the majority was too credulous in accepting the government's claim that national security was imperiled. National security is never at risk in such matters but governments, whether Democratic or Republican, find it an irresistible argument.

Meanwhile the court, ever hostile to cameras in the courtroom, halted telecasting of a same-sex trial in San Francisco. It's an issue that needs light, not court-imposed darkness.

The 2009-2010 term did have one standout decision: it ruled that juveniles who commit crimes in which no one was killed cannot be sentenced to life in prison.

In a concurring opinion, Justice Stevens wrote: "Punishment that did not seem cruel and unusual at one time may in the light of reason be found cruel and unusual at a later time."

This was too much for the great 14th century mind of Justice Thomas. He lamented that the only cruel and unusual punishment was torture.

On the positive side, the court asked Georgia to reconsider the death sentence of an innocent man. Nevertheless, the dissenting troglodytes, Justice Scalia and Thomas, insisted that the court has no duty to prevent the death of someone who is innocent.

In another case the heartless duo dissented when the court said a man could not be sentenced to death just becase his lawyer missed a filing deadine. The law is the law, the merciless ones insisted--even when the law is an ass.

On a happier note, the newest justice, Sonia Sotomayor, spoke glowingly in dissent about a suspect's Miranda rights. Unfortunately she was outvoted by the Five Horsemen of Reaction.

Justices rarely rise above their background and biases. Former Justice Brennan was a wonderful exception. He sided with the majority declaring abortion legal even though Brennan was a regular Mass-attending Catholic.

In contrast, take the five Catholics on the court today: Chief Justice Roberts and his fellow politicians, Justices Scalia, Thomas, Kennedy and Alito. They consistently vote against Vatican insistence on social justice for all.

Sparks Tribune, July 11, 2010

Return of robber baronism

The Supreme Court, confirming the fact that the dollar rules everything in American politics, has declared once again that money is speech.

In other words, the 7 million American millionaires have greater free speech than 275 million ordinary folks. The millionaires can take out multiple full-page ads in newspapers and buy expensive TV spots. The vast majority of Americans cannot afford such First Amendment "freedom."

The ruling unmasks any pretense that America is a democracy. It re-emphasizes that the Roberts Court is utterly pro-business and pro-Republican.

Grant Leneaux, Western tradition professor at the University of Nevada, Reno, called the decision what it was: "the legally sanctioned triumph of plutocratic capitalism."

The New York Times observed caustically: "The Supreme Court has thrust politics back to the Robber Baron era of the 19th century. Disingenuously waving the flag of the First Amendment, the court's conservative majority has paved the way for corporations to use their vast treasuries to win elections and intimidate elected officials into doing their bidding."

And columnist E.J. Dionne denounced the decision as "an astonishing display of judicial arrogance, overreach and unjustified activism."

For decades right-wingers complained about judicial activism when the Warren Court was ruling for people not property. But the real judicial activism long has come from the judicial right--to the great detriment of the nation.

Justice Stevens wrote a 90-page dissent laced with outrage and sarcasm.

He said the majority had made "a grave error in putting

corporate speech on the same level as people speech," that the majority had "blazed through the court's precedents" to overrule or disavow "a body of case law."

"The difference between selling a vote and selling access is a matter of degree, not kind," Stevens said. "And selling access is not qualitatively different from giving special preference to those who spent money on one's behalf."

The decision in Citizens United v. Federal Election Commission corrupts democracy. It allows corporations to dominate the marketplace of ideas.

As long ago as 1809 the Supreme Court said that corporations are "a mere legal entity," not people. In 1946 the court made the same point: "corporations are not entitled to all of the constitutional protections that private individuals have."

The ruling is a scathing indictment of the Roberts Court. The court denied First Amendment protection to a harmless and humorous banner unfurled by an Alaskan high school kid but gave First Amendment protection to powerful and baleful corporations.

The Roberts Court is the modern version of the Five Horseman of Reaction that plagued the country in the 1930s. Its Citizens United ruling joins two other odious decisions in Supreme Court history, Dred Scott and Bush v. Gore.

The Dred Scott ruling by the Taney Court in 1857 said blacks were inferior beings who "had no rights which the white man was bound to respect." It also allowed slavery to be extended to the territories.

Bush v. Gore, decided by the Rehnquist Court in 2000, stopped the Florida vote recount to rob Al Gore of the presidency. Again Stevens angrily dissented. He rightly pointed out the obvious: the court is not an "impartial guardian of the rule of law."

Moreover, the reactionary judicial activists on the Roberts Court are likely to decide the law of the land for decades, thwarting even mildly liberal presidents and "vetoing" any progressive measures.

Frank Rich, New York Times essay journalist, notes sourly: the decision gives corporations "an even greater stranglehold over a government they already regard as a partially owned offshore subsidiary."

The Nation continues the denunciation, citing the 1990 ruling by the Supreme Court in the Austin case which lambasted "the corrosive and distorting effects of immense aggregations of corporate wealth."

Justice Byron White, hardly a radical except in the perfervid minds of right-wingers, dissented in the 1978 Bellotti corporate advertising case.

White said corporations had an unfair advantage in the political process. "The communications of profitmaking corporations are not an integral part of the development of ideas or mental exploration and of the affirmation of self."

At his confirmation hearing, Roberts said the job of a justice was simply "to call balls and strikes and not to pitch or bat." As chief justice, however, Roberts is pitching and batting.

No close follower of the court believed Roberts' pretense of impartiality. As a Washington corporate lawyer he made $1 million a year. After his court's enormous gift to corporations, Roberts had been woefully underpaid.

Sparks Tribune, Feb. 7, 2010

Top court denies justice

The façade of the Supreme Court building proclaims: "Equal Justice for All." But the Roberts Court metes out justice for just some.

Lady Justice is blind but she shouldn't be deaf and dumb too. The most egregious decision in the 2008-2009 court term: rejection of the right of prisoners to DNA testing to prove their innocence.

Chief Justice Roberts admitted as much in his opinion for the court, noting the unparalled ability of DNA evidence to prove innocence.

But in one of the most bizarre rationales in the history of the court, Roberts said that this does not mean that "every criminal conviction involving biological evidence is in doubt."

The five reactionaries interpret the Constitution as they want: let defendants be electrocuted. As Justice Stevens said in dissent: "There is no reason to deny access to the evidence and there are many reasons to provide it."

Another lamentable decision by the Backward Five eroded the exclusionary rule prohibiting prosecutors from using evidence obtained in an improper police search.

It was an un-American decision. Justice Holmes in a dissent in Olmstead (1928) knew what it meant to be an American. He wrote: it is a lesser evil "that some criminals should escape than that the government should play an ignoble part."

The Baleful Five also undermined the Sixth Amendment right to counsel, declaring it wasn't always essential. Stevens bitterly dissented, correctly declaring that defendants must have counsel at every stage of prosecution.

In all three cases the vote was 5-4. In each case Justice Kennedy was the fifth man. Kennedy is the most powerful jurist in America, so often determining the law of the land. But being powerful doesn't mean dispensing justice.

The Supreme Court constantly overrules decisions by the U.S. Circuit Court of Appeals for the 9th Circuit, the most liberal court in America, Unfortunately, the reactionary Supreme Court has the last word.

And that means environmentalists lost all five cases, including the undercutting of the Clean Water Act to allow a company to fill an Alaskan lake with mine waste. Kennedy, writing for the majority, said deference must be accorded the company. Justice Ginsburg shot back in dissent: what about paying deference to the Clean Water Act?

In another dreadful ruling, the Five Horsemen of Reaction weakened legal protection against age discrimination. An anguished Stevens acidly dissented: "I disagree not only with the court's interpretation of the statute but also with its decision to engage in lawmaking."

In another despicable opinion, the Puritanical Five backed the FCC ban on airwaves expletives. Justice Scalia in his opinion for the court denounced the words fuck and shit uttered by Cher in a televised awards ceremony. (The priggish Scalia played the silly newspaper game of referring to the f-word and s-word.)

Scalia should read the dissent by Justice Brennan in FCC v. Pacifica (1978): "There are many who think, act and talk differently from the members of this court and who do not share their fragile sensibilities. It is only an acute ethnocentric myopia that enables the court to approve the censorship of communications solely because of the words they contain."

Expletives deserve First Amendment protection. Stevens in dissent noted the irony of curbing harmless four-letter words while allowing commercials for Viagra, Cialis and Levitra.

On the positive side, the strip search of an Arizona middle school girl was ruled unconstitutional. Justice Souter, writing for an 8-1 court, called it "embarrassing, frightening and humiliating."

Dissenting Justice Thomas, clinging to the law of the past, said public schools must preserve "order, discipline and safety." Troglodyte Thomas is probably the worst justice in history. He certainly is the most archreactionary.

Learned Hand, one of the best judges who never reached the Supreme Court, said he would open every session of court with the words of Cromwell: "I beseech you, in the bowels of Christ, to think it possible you may be mistaken."

Justice Brandeis made the same point. Dissenting in the obscure 1932 New State Ice case, Brandeis warned the court about its enormous power of judicial review: "In the exercise of this high power we must be ever on our guard lest we erect our prejudices into legal principles."

But that is precisely what the Supreme Court has been doing for decades, making its biases legal principles.

Sparks Tribune, July 12, 2009

Partisan reality of top court

THE NINE. Inside the Secret World of the Supreme Court. By Jeffrey Toobin, 411 pages, Anchor Paperback, 2008.

Supreme Court nomination hearings have become a game of charades. The senators preen and pontificate and the nominees are evasive and disingenuous.

When nominee Sonia Sotomayor was grilled recently, a senator asked: "Can you be objective?"

Sure, she said, in an appeasing way. But she should have replied: "As objective as Chief Justice Roberts and Justices Scalia, Kennedy, Thomas and Alito."

Such an answer, while true, would not have been politic. But the Reactionary Five is hardly objective. It is as partisan as any politician.

Roberts, in his nomination hearing, said "judges are not politicians" but simply umpires.

Malarkey.

Judge Learned Hand, one of America's best jurists, who never served on the Supreme Court, observed: "It is the way of judges to disguise what they are doing and impute to it a derivative far more imperative than their personal preferences, which are all that lie behind their decisions."

And Chief Justice Hughes told a young Justice Douglas when he joined the court: "At the constitutional level where we work, ninety percent of any decision is emotional. The rationale part of us supplies the reasons for supporting our predilections."

After the egregious Bush v. Gore decision in 2000, former Justice Souter called the majority opinion what it was: crudely partisan.

The Toobin look, an inside look at the Supreme Court, tells similar truths as "The Brethren" did. Written by

Bob Woodward and Scott Armstrong 20 years ago, "The Brethren" described Chief Justice Burger as the "pompous, egomaniacal and bumbler" he was.

Toobin's frankness is in the same vein. He writes:

• Former Justice O'Connor, no radical, called G.W. Bush "arrogant, lawless, incompetent and extreme."

• Justice Kennedy has "a weakness for high-flown, sometimes meaningless rhetoric."

• Justice Stevens is "dignified, clear-headed, his eloquence honors the court."

• Justice Scalia displays juvenile impetulance, calling people idiots when they disagree with his originalist view of the Constitution.

• Justice Thomas, a "white black," is so retrograde that just one of his first 40 clerks was black.

Sparks Tribune, Jan. 10, 2010

Justice Souter: retiring star

Justice David Souter could probably walk into a popular Washington, D.C., restaurant and not be recognized by 49 out of 50 diners.

In this celebrity-conscious land, the Supreme Court justices rank well below Britney Spears, Paris Hilton and Homer Simpson in public recognition. The Supreme Court itself is a virtually unknown body unless it hands down decisions stirring outrage on issues like abortion and flag-burning.

Souter will happily retire this summer, going counter to the dictum of Jefferson that few in power die and none resign.

Souter had no flash, no dash, no flamboyance. He was quiet and unassuming. But he was a sterling man and a fine justice. He was decent and humane, so unlike the Five Horsemen of Reaction who control the court today.

Souter refused to join the court politicians who turn their prejudices into legal principles. He refused to join them in ruling for corporations, property and business. He chose the side of the angels: people, consumers and justice.

Adam Liptak, Supreme Court reporter for the New York Times, has written supercilious stories declaring that Souter was a careful, "a low-impact justice." Liptak compounded the insults by writing that Justice Scalia has a judicial philosophy while Souter has none, that Scalia is highly quotable while Souter is not.

Memo to Establishment journalist Liptak: 50 Scalias are not worth one Souter.

The Supreme Court has had 110 justices. None wrote as well as Oliver Wendell Holmes whose opinions are studded with aphorisms and wonderful philosophical asides. Most of the justices have been poor writers, including the outstanding Justice Brennan. Most of them wrote too long except for the blessed brevity of Justices Holmes, Black and Douglas.

But what counts is decisions, not how well justices write or how much they are quoted.

Perhaps Souter's most memorable decision was Casey, reaffirming the constitutional right to abortion. In another memorable case, Souter joined the majority in upholding the sacred right of habeas corpus. He led the court in reversal of a black man's conviction of killing a white woman because the jury was nearly all white. He cast the pivotal fifth vote to uphold affirmative action.

But it was in dissent that Souter stood out. When the court upheld the notorious three-strikes-and-you're-out law, Souter dissented. He noted the absurdity of sending a man to jail for life for a third felony like stealing a golf bag.

He dissented when the court struck down the Violence Against Women Act, calling the ruling a woeful misreading of the Constitution. When the economic royalists killed the overtime pay provision of the Labor Standards Act, Souter dissented. He denounced the violation of civil liberties and equal protection.

When the court killed a provision of the Americans with Disabilities Act, Souter complained in dissent about the court's "crabbed version" of the law. When the court upheld a law requiring the National Endowment of the Arts to take into account so-called decency, he rightly dissented.

He was dismayed when the court overturned an effort by schools in Louisville, Ky., to prevent resegregation. His dissent called the ruling profoundly unhistorical.

When the court ruled that public schools must be open to Bible study groups, Souter dissented because of the clear violation of the wall between church and state. When the Unholy Five smashed that wall by saying that the University of Virginia must subsidize an evangelical magazine, Souter dissented. He decried the violation of the First Amendment in approval of state funding for religion.

However, Souter was clearly wrong about one thing: cameras in the Supreme Court. He insisted that "the day you see a camera coming into our courtroom it's going to roll over my dead body."

The courtroom is a sacred place. But the "nine old men" adamantly refuse to enter the Digital Age. The Supreme Court is an appellate court. It studies the facts and decisions of lower courts.

Unlike jurors, the justices are not persuaded by emotions, by the tricks and pyrotechnics of trial lawyers. The Supreme Court deals with substantive constitutional issues. It would enlighten citizens to see and hear the oral arguments presenting the pros and cons of an issue, the fierce questioning by the justices.

Skelly Wright, the late, great appeals court judge, rightly argued that televising oral arguments would "be a matchless lesson in the meaning of our constitutional rights and principles."

Justice is supposed to be blind--but not invisible.

Finally, a confession. I wrote after Souter's appointment that nothing in his background indicated he would rise above mediocrity. So much for the omniscience of columnists!

Souter had a marvelous capacity for growth, a quality alien to the "brilliant" Scalia. Souter became a bright star among a dim constellation of reactionaries.

Sparks Tribune, May 17, 2009

Dissenter Stevens outgrew GOP

Justice Stevens is the near Great Dissenter on the Supreme Court today.

Near great because, while he has given some impassioned dissents, he has also issued a few lamentable opinions.

Stevens, who will retire this summer, dissented more than 600 times in his 34 years on the bench. He rose above his Republican roots, growing in wisdom to lead the court's liberal bloc.

Stevens is a humanistic judge in a institution saddled with mossbacks utterly devoid of compassion. Those reactionaries are pro-corporation, pro-business, pro-prosecution, pro-government, pro-wealth, pro-discrimination, pro-pollution and pro-white.

Stevens was right to dissent in these major cases:

• He got apoplectic in an 88-page dissent denouncing the Five Horsemen of Reaction who blithely made corporations people and money speech. Stevens said of the 2010 decision in Citizens United: "While American democracy is imperfect, few outside the majority of this court would have thought its flaws included a dearth of corporate money in politics."

• He dissented from the outrageous political decision in 2000 that gave the presidency to G.W. Bush. "The loser is perfectly clear," he wrote. "It is the nation's confidence in the judge as an impartial guardian of the rule of law."

• He shook his head in disbelief in 2007 when the court, in effect, overturned Brown v. Board of Education, killing a Seattle school integration plan. The court had moved Right. He had not moved Left.

• Stevens dissented when the court allowed Boy Scouting to bar gays. Calling the decision mind-boggling,

Stevens said the court made discrimination law and homosexuals a symbol of inferiority.

• Stevens dissented from the court ruling in 2008 overturning a gun control law in the District of Columbia. He sarcastically noted that the majority "would have us believe that...the Framers made a choice to limit the tools available to elected officials wishing to regulate civilian uses of weapons."

• Stevens in the Snepp case (1981) saw through the White House subterfuge that national security was at stake in the CIA's secrecy agreement with its agents. Stevens noted in his dissent that Snepp's book about the fall of Saigon contained no classified information.

Writing for the majority, Stevens rejected in Rasul (2004) the notion that the president was above the law, that Bush could rule by executive authority. Stevens wrote for the majority in Hamdan (2006) that military commissions violated the Geneva Conventions.

He joined the majority in Lawrence v. Texas (2003) overturning legislation barring sodomy, nullifying a horrible decision by the court. In that earlier ruling (Hardwick) the court upheld a Georgia anti-sodomy law over Stevens' dissent.

But Stevens was wrong in these major cases:

• Texas v. Johnson (1989). Stevens read from the bench, his face red and his eyes brimmed with tears. He said the flag was a symbol of everything the nation stands for. Because he was a Navy vet in World War II, he was unable to see the constitutional question: the right to burn the flag as symbolic protest speech.

Stevens' showed that he was a metaphorical Old Man in 1978 when he wrote the majority view upholding a broadcast ban on George Carlin's "seven dirty words" monologue.

Stevens had a failure of nerve in Baze (2008). He

rightly said executions are "patently excessive and unusual punishment violative of the Eight Amendment." But he gutlessly upheld lethal injection because of precedent.

Stevens egregiously voted to uphold voter ID in an Indiana case (2008), declaring in a majority opinion that the law stopped voter fraud. Voting fraud is almost nonexistent. The law aims to keep Democrats from the polls.

It was yet another political decision by an extremely political Supreme Court.

Chief Justice Roberts complained that the State of the Union speech had "degenerated to a political rally." Roberts should know. He constantly injects right-wing politics into court rulings.

Holmes, often called the Great Dissenter, also had some outrageous opinions sprinkled among these great dissents: Abrams: "we should be eternally vigilant against attempts to check the expression of opinions that we loathe"; Olmstead: "I think it a less evil that some criminals should escape than that the government (federal agents) should play an ignoble part"); and Lochner: dissenting from the court's decision in 1905 to strike down a 10-hour day for bakers "The Fourteenth Amendment does not enact Mr. Herbert Spencer's 'Social Statics' " (a reactionary screed).

On the down side, Holmes upheld Alabama racist laws, considered Eugene Debs a common criminal, confused dissent in wartime with disloyalty and, upholding sterilization, said "three generations of imbeciles are enough."

Nevertheless, Stevens and Holmes rank among the 10 best justices in Supreme Court history. Stevens believed with Holmes that constitutional law must respond to the "felt necessities of the times."

Sparks Tribune, April 25, 2010

Sotomayor's 'crime': liberalism

Benighted Republican senators, angry because President Obama did not pick a Genghis Khan or an Attila the Hun for the Supreme Court, have trained their ire on poor Judge Sonia Sotomayor.

Her crime? A smattering of liberalism in her decisions on the 2nd U.S. Circuit Court of Appeals.

Never mind that the Supreme Court is already packed with reactionaries, constantly voting 5-4, 5-4, 5-4, to strike down anything decent and humane and to uphold anything indecent and inhumane.

Jeffrey Toobin, in a recent New Yorker article, limned the Five Horsemen of Reaction led by Chief Justice Roberts. It sides "with the prosecution over the defendant, the state over the condemned, the executive branch over the legislature and the corporate defendant over the individual plaintiff." It defers "to the existing power relationships in society."

Justice Souter nailed Roberts when dissenting from an opinion the chief justice wrote. Souter said Roberts' opinion reminded him of Anatole France's observation that "the law, in its majestic equality, forbids the rich as well as the poor to sleep under bridges, to beg in the streets and to steal bread."

Obama as an Illinois senator voted against confirmation of Roberts, correctly declaring that Roberts uses "his formidable skills on behalf of the strong in opposition to the weak."

"I will seek someone who understands that justice isn't about some abstract legal theory or footnote in a casebook," Obama said. "It is also about how our laws affect the daily realities of people's lives."

Which is where Judge Sotomayor is perfect. She understands the struggles of so many Americans. Roberts in his ivory tower and smug comfort will never understand that reality.

Sotomayor was born in the Bronx, New York, to Puerto Rican parents. She was brought up in a housing project, providing the empathy that Obama seeks.

However, her understanding of the Little People gets her into trouble with GOP troglodytes. In a 2001 speech, Sotomayor said: "a wise Latina with the richness of her experiences would more often than not reach a better conclusion than a white male who hasn't lived that life."

She is being reviled as racist for speaking the truth. Roberts, in contrast, epitomizes nearly all lawyers and judges: howling conservatives.

Supreme Court history is full of reactionary decisions favoring business and property against the needs of people and the humanism of civilized nations. It has so often blinked at reality and found its retrograde politics in the Constitution.

Just a few examples among so many: 1) Dred Scott [1857] held that slaves were property, inferior beings and "had no rights the white man was bound to respect." 2) In Adkins [1923] the court struck down a Washington, D.C., minimum wage.

3) In Coppage v. Kansas [1915] the court called yellow-dog contracts--forced vows not to join a union--constitutional. The court gleefully noted that "some people have more property than others," "the right of private property" was paramount and that "inequalities of fortune" are just.

4) In Hammer v. Dagenhart [1918] the court declared child labor constitutional. 5) In two years it struck down 10 major New Deal laws--judicial nullification without parallel in U.S. history. 6) In Bush v. Gore [2000] the court, in a partisan political decision that had nothing to

do with the law, stopped the Florida recount to hand the presidency to G.W. Bush.

Sotomayor would bring much more to the court then mere knowledge of the underside of life. She is smart, compassionate and thoughtful.

Roberts, at 54 a young man as Supreme Court justices go, could plague the country for decades. But at least Sotomayor would inject the same compassion shown by Justices Stevens, Ginsburg and Souter in their heated dissents.

On the appeals bench, Sotomayor ruled for baseball players, not the owners. She ruled that homeless people must be paid the minimum wage. She held that an inmate could sue a corporation operating a halfway house for federal prisoners.

She ruled that a broker who held stocks because of misleading information could sue. She wrote that the Environmental Protection Agency cannot use cost-benefit calculations to preserve aquatic species.

She dissented when her appeals court upheld the legality of strip searches for girls at a juvenile detention center in Connecticut. She called it what it was: embarrassing and humiliating.

Nevertheless, Sotomayor is hardly a flaming liberal. She was wrong to side with New Haven, Conn., when it rejected results of a firefighter promotion test because blacks and Latinos performed poorly. Her abortion position is unclear, having decided few pro-choice cases and all those on the fringes of Roe.

But no justice ever scores 100 percent. Sotomayor is a good choice to replace the retiring Souter.

Sparks Tribune, June 7, 2009

Kagan milquetoast nominee

The trouble with Elena Kagan is that she is a lawyer. Indeed, one big trouble with the Supreme Court justices is that they are *all* lawyers.

What the court needs is a labor leader, a man or a woman who understands what work is. The court's lawyers constantly issue pro-business decisions. They often have done so throughout history, notably during the 1930s when the court systematically struck down the New Deal.

The court also needs a woman like writer Barbara Ehrenreich who went undercover to point out that she needed three jobs, all low-paying, to buy food and pay the rent.

Kagan, nominated to the court by President Obama, is bright as you would expect of a Harvard law school grad and dean.

But she is an Ivy Leaguer, like the rest of the court, with little understanding of how most people live. (Harvard leads Yale on the court, 5-3. Kagan's confirmation would make it 6-3.)

To paraphrase the Bill Buckley quip: better to have Supreme Court decisions made by the first one hundred people listed in the Boston phone directory than by Harvardites.

Kagan thinks like a lawyer: prudent, cautious and conservative. She is a careerist, a calculator, figuring how to get to the top of Disraeli's greasy pole. She often suffers "amnesia," declaring that she does not "recall ever expressing an opinion" on many controversies.

Her record indicates little passion about anything except the notorious military bias against gays and lesbians. She called the don't ask, don't tell policy "a profound wrong, a moral injustice." (The fact that Kagan is a lesbian probably accounts for her justified outrage.)

Above all else, Kagan is confirmable. That's why Obama appointed her. He could have chosen people like Laurence Tribe, Harvard law professor, but he's too liberal. Or he could have picked Stephen Reinhardt of the 9th Circuit in San Francisco, the best U.S. appeals court judge in America. But he is too progressive.

Obama, too, is a lawyer. Pragmatic. Which means conservative. He plays it safe. He settles for the passable rather than the best.

Yet the point must be made again and again: you can never tell about a nominee. Once on the court justices are independent. They are not beholden to anyone.

President Teddy Roosevelt picked Oliver Wendell Holmes because he thought Holmes favored his trust-busting campaign. Holmes quickly disabused him.

FDR chose Felix Frankfurter because Frankfurter had fought the good liberal fight for Sacco-Vanzetti. On the court Frankfurter became a conservative.

Republican President Eisenhower picked Earl Warren and Bill Brennan. Ike ruefully said later that they were the only two mistakes he made as president.

Conservative Republican presidents appointed John Paul Stevens and David Souter but as justices they drifted to liberalism

Nevertheless, Kagan's public positions are not encouraging. They carry the musty odor of conservatism. She was a clerk for Justice Thurgood Marshall when the court upheld a school busing fee for poor families.

Marshall vigorously dissented, noting acidly: "The intent of our 14th Amendment was to abolish caste legislation."

Later Kagan complained that Marshall had "allowed his personal experiences and the knowledge of suffering and deprivation gained from these experiences to guide him."

But what else logically would guide his jurisprudence? Marshall felt the sting and knew the injustice of black discrimination. He fought valiantly--and historically--against prejudice. He was *not* an Ivy League lawyer.

Kagan? Her family could afford to send her to elitist and expensive Princeton and abroad to study at Oxford.

As Clinton's deputy domestic adviser, Kagan backed the bogus reform that kicked off the rolls poor women and single mothers. As dean of Harvard law school, she had a right-wing agenda for faculty appointments: 25 white men, six white women and one Asian woman.

Several of the hires were prominent in the reactionary Federalist Society. Not one hire was black, Latino or Native American. For three years she was a paid adviser to Goldman Sachs, hedge fund masters of financial legerdemain.

Kagan in her confirmation hearings to be solicitor general declared: "There is no constitutional right to same-sex marriage." In those same hearings she defended the ever-widening unconstitutional executive power of the president at home and abroad.

Still, senators for the Party of No will complain that Kagan has no judicial experience. An absurd argument, belied by history. Many justices, including Warren, the greatest U.S. chief justice, never were judges.

But Warren knew instinctively the proper role of the court: "Where there is injustice, we should correct it." He placed people over property, a concept alien to the retrograde lawyers ruling the Supreme Court today.

Sparks Tribune, May 23, 2010

Property over people

The pro-business bias of the Supreme Court was clearly laid out in a recent article in the New York Times Magazine. It was aptly titled: Supreme Court Inc.

Yet the article by Jeffrey Rosen was hardly surprising. Law schools inculcate conservatism. Lawyers, judges and law professors are overwhelmingly conservative. They have been swept into the Big Business orbit and the mania for rampant capitalism.

As the late Milton Friedman, the conservatives' favorite economist, pointed out, lawyers are the guardians of free-market capitalism.

Exceptions prove the rule. Justices Brandeis, Holmes, Black, Douglas and Brennan have been certified liberals. Brandeis was a people's justice but naturally conservatives complained that he was a socialist and hence un-American. Douglas was such an economic populist that he was "ready to bend the law in favor of the environment and against the corporations."

But the vast majority of the 111 justices in history have been conservative. They have put property over people. That's why the late, lamented Warren Court was the best court ever. It put people over property.

Even the social liberals on today's Roberts Court are conservatives in business cases. They doubt the validity of lawsuits challenging corporate wrong-doing, what conservatives call "regulation by litigation."

These court rulings, as Jim Hightower phrased it in his Lowdown newsletter, allow "owners to reap all the profits of corporate activity while they are protected from any responsibility for corporate illegalities."

In the 2006-2007 term the U.S. Chamber of Commerce, powerful lobbying force for business, filed briefs in 15 cases. It won 13. Of 30 business cases decided last term,

22 were decided unanimously or with only one or two dissents.

Business cases, in which the arguments are often abstruse, get little attention as opposed to inflaming issues like abortion, the death penalty and affirmative action.

But as Rosen notes of business cases: "They involve billions of dollars, have huge consequences for the economy and can have a greater effect on people's daily lives than the often symbolic battles of the culture wars."

Already this term the Roberts Court has ruled, 8-1, that makers of medical devices like heart defibrillators and implants cannot be sued for personal injuries if the FDA approved the devices.

A New York Times editorial noted that the decision written by Justice Scalia showed far too much faith in the FDA. "The supposedly expert and rigorous reviewers at the FDA are hardly infallible," the editorial said. It cited many reports of "serious defects in the agency's management and scientific capabilities."

The decision lends support to the Rosen thesis. It also underscores the success of regulatory agencies in the Bush administration to protect corporations at the expense of aggrieved citizens.

But how could it be otherwise? Chief Justice Roberts once argued cases for the Chamber of Commerce. He was described glowingly as the "go-to lawyer for the business community." (Forty years earlier Justice Lewis Powell had been a corporate lawyer.)

Two other court decisions this term show pro-business bias. In one, the court refused to allow a shareholder suit against suppliers of Charter Communications. In the second, the court refused to hear an appeal in which investors are trying to recover $40 billion from Wall Street banks that aided the Enron fraud.

It has always been thus.

Thomas Cooley, a Michigan judge and law professor, was highly influential in the 1860s with his "Treatise on Constitutional Limits." He argued that "legislative enactment is not necessarily the law of the land" and that state laws to curb business excesses were interfering with liberty and property.

In 1894 President Cleveland sent federal troops to bust the Pullman Car railway strike, wrecking the union. Strike leader Eugene Debs was arrested on a charge of contempt. Thousands of strikers were blacklisted.

Thus, Social Darwinism reigned in the 1880s and 1890s with judges striking down hundreds of state laws. The reign continued into the 20th century. In 1905 the court killed a law limiting the working day of bakers to 10 hours, provoking a stinging dissent from Holmes that the Fourteenth Amendment (due process) does not enact Herbert Spencer's reactionary policies.

After the court ruled in 1918 that a law barring child labor was unconstitutional, socialist Debs denounced the decision as allowing the "junkers of Wall Street" to "grind the flesh and blood and bones of puny little children into profits." And Holmes excoriated the majority for intruding its personal judgments into "questions of policy and morals."

In business matters the elite justices triumph over the will of a vast majority of Americans. They are economic royalists backing the evils of capitalism.

Sparks Tribune, April 13, 2008

Court and corporatocracy

It speaks volumes about the Supreme Court when it could not rule on a case recently because it lacked a quorum of six.

Three justices recused themselves because they held stock in companies being litigated. A fourth justice recused himself because his son works for one of the firms.

Embarrassing, yes. But it shows that the justices are rich and therefore seldom rule for the vast majority of people.

Seven members of the court are millionaires. Justice Kennedy, poor fellow, has a net worth of just $750,000. Weep too for Justice Thomas who has gotten just $1 million in book advances since 2003.

Earlier this year Chief Justice Roberts recused himself in a drug case because he owns stock in Pfizer, the parent company of a defendant in the litigation. This resulted in a 4-4 decision, upholding the pro-business ruling of the appeals court.

The same thing could happen when the court soon hands down a decision on the damage suit against Exxon in the Valdez oil spill. Justice Alito recused himself because he owns stock in Exxon.

Executive branch officials are required to divest themselves of stocks that could be a conflict of interest. Not the justices. They are a law unto themselves.

The Supreme Court is the least known branch of government. That's why few people realize that it is very much a part of the corporatocracy ruling America, the unholy triumvirate of corporations, banks and government.

The court made clear its preference for that corporatocracy when it ruled in April that the Indiana voter photo identification law was constitutional.

In effect, the decision restored the poll tax, designed

to hold down black votes in the South, which the Supreme Court had abolished four decades ago. The ruling also nullified the 24th Amendment which prohibits poll taxes.

The Indiana law, upheld 6-3, requires citizens to show a photo ID at the polls, either a driver's license or a passport. The decision reverses two centuries of jurisprudence declaring a voter signature sufficent ID.

The majority opinion, fracturing logic, was written by Justice Stevens, once a liberal but now becoming senile at 88 and returning to his GOP roots. He claimed the risk of voter fraud is real.

Palpable nonsense. Voter fraud is so rare as to be nonexistent. The truth is that photo ID is part of a concerted effort by Republican state lawmakers to prevent blacks, Latinos and the elderly from voting.

Why? They tend to vote Democratic. The court ruling has prompted 20 states to seek enactment of photo ID statutes.

Up to 13 percent of Indiana voters, most of them Democrats, will be ineligible to vote for lack of photo ID. Indeed, about 20 million Americans do not have a driver's license bearing a photo.

In dissent, Justice Souter saw through the chicanery. He said the photo ID requirement was a serious burden, one that Indiana had not justified.

Comparing photo ID to the poll tax struck down by the Supreme Court in 1966, Souter said: "the onus of the Indiana law is illegitimate because it correlates with no state interest so well as it does with the object of deterring poorer residents from exercising the franchise."

The New York Times noted the irony of the ID decision: "Seven years after it invoked the Constitution to vindicate what it saw as President Bush's right to fair election procedures, we are still waiting for the court to extend this guarantee with equal vigilance to every American."

Illegal immigrants voting? Ridiculous. As illegals, they would hardly risk exposure by trying to vote. However, vigilant officials did stop a subversive group from voting in the Indiana primary this year: a group of nuns without voter ID!

Driving down the voter turnout will help the corporatocracy rule in perpetuity. Keeping the poor, the elderly, racial minorities and college students--who are wild about Obama--from voting fosters that sinister design.

The head of the Republican Party in Alabama has admitted that the Republicans object to restoring voting rights of former felons "because felons don't tend to vote Republican."

Positions are taken in politics, not because they are right, but because of partisan advantage.

America is far from the great democracy it boasts of being. Bush brags about the wonders of voting in Afghanistan and Iraq while his party denies the franchise to voters who do not have a driver's license.

This is the reactionary Supreme Court that gave us eight years of the Bush stain and is now ruling so McCain can continue that imperial, unconstitutional reign.

Sparks Tribune, June 15, 2008

Court invokes rule of law

John Adams, second president, popularized the words enshrined in the Massachusetts Constititution: "A government of laws not men." G.W. Bush, 43rd president, reversed that truism to the great detriment of the American people.

A perfect example of that reversal is found in the arrogant attitude of Vice President Cheney. He was being interviewed by Martha Raddatz of ABC. She noted that two-thirds of the American people thought that the war in Iraq was not worth fighting.

"*So?*" Cheney asked.

"*So?* You don't care what the American people think?"

"No."

Cheney doesn't care but the Supreme Court does. Three times since 2004 it has rebuked the lawless Bush administration with ringing declarations that this is a nation of laws not men.

The latest decision, Boumediene v. Bush, declared that prisoners held at Guantánamo have a constitutional right to challenge their detention in U.S. courts.

Habeas corpus, the Great Writ, still rules despite the efforts of Bush to quash it.

The roots of habeas corpus go back nine centuries to England. Its rudiments can be found in the Magna Carta of 1215 when barons at Runnymede forced King John to yield some of his arbitrary power. Habeas corpus was codified by Parliament in 1679.

In America, habeas corpus has been considered legally holy. It has been called "the most important human right in the Constitution." Chief Justice Chase declared in a 1868 ruling that habeas was "the best and only sufficent defense of personal freedom."

In a 1963 case, Justice Brennan was absolutely ecstatic about the writ. He wrote:

"Its history is inextricably intertwined with the growth of fundamental rights of personal liberty. For its function has been to provide a prompt and efficacious remedy for whatever society deems to be intolerable restraints. Its root principle is that in a civilized society government must always be accountable to the judiciary for a man's imprisonment."

Justice Kennedy, who wrote the majority opinion in Boumediene, said that liberty and security must be reconciled "within the framework of the law," that President Bush cannot "switch the Constitution on or off at will." He added:

"Within the Constitution's separation of powers few exercises of judicial power are as legitimate or as necessary as the responsibility to hear challenges to the authority of the executive to imprison a person,"

Many of the 270 Guantánamo prisoners have been held for six years without charges. Geoffrey Stone, University of Chicago law professor, said Bush "has made extreme claims that are lawfully and constitutionally unfounded."

But to dissenting Chief Justice Roberts, the Great Writ is nothing more than "a procedural right."

Another dissenter, the reactionary Justice Scalia, complained of the majority's "inflated notion of judicial supremacy" and declared that the ruling "will almost certainly cause more Americans to be killed." Scalia is the same despicable justice who told BBC in February that torture may sometimes be justified.

Scalia, a supposedly brilliant guy, speaks an infinite deal of nonsense. He concluded his dissent by declaring that "the court warps our Constitution" and that the nation "will live to regret" the decision.

Scalia is a sorry excuse for a justice on a court that once had giants like Brandeis, Holmes, Warren, Murphy, Black and Douglas.

A New York Times editorial praised the Boumediene decision and denounced the "imperial overreaching" of Bush. It noted:

"With the help of compliant Republicans and frightened Democrats in Congress, President Bush has denied the protections of justice, democracy and plain human decency to the hundreds of men that he decided to label 'unlawful enemy combatants' and throw into never-ending detention."

Columnist Eugene Robinson, noting that Bush had put a "chainsaw to the rule of law," wrote that he was amazed that there was anything to debate about "arbitrary arrest, indefinite detention and torture."

Bush also put a chainsaw to the Constitution, international treaties and the military code of justice.

Few people know what it means to be a true American, to be a real patriot. It is *not* wearing a flag pin. It is *not* flying the flag.

No. It is words like these by Holmes dissenting in Olmstead (1928): "For my part I think it is less evil that some criminals should escape than that the government should play an ignoble part."

Or those by Brandeis dissenting in Olmstead: "Our government is the potent, the omnipresent teacher...it teaches the whole people by its example. If the government becomes a lawbreaker, it breeds contempt for the law."

Or these by Murphy dissenting in In Re Yamashita (1946): "The immutable rights of the individual...belong to every person on the world."

Sparks Tribune, July 6, 2008

Courts dent gay bias

Intolerance. Hatred. Bigotry. Prejudice. Discrimination. Ignorance. Fear. All were dealt a severe blow by the courts as gays and lesbians recently won two sparkling victories.

One declared the right of same-sex couples to marry and the other portended the end of the military's absurd policy of "don't ask, don't tell."

The California Supreme Court struck down state laws that had limited marriage to a union between men and women. And, a three-judge panel of the 9th U.S. Circuit Court of Appeals reinstated a suit against the Air Force, declaring that the military cannot discharge people because they are gay.

In the gay marriage case, Chief Justice Ron George wrote for the majority: "In view of…the fundamental constitutional right to form a family relationship, the California Constitution…guarantees this basic civil right to all Californians."

The ruling gives gay couples the benefits and protections of hetrosexual marriage. They can get tax and insurance benefits and the right to family leaves and hospital visits.

An editorial in the San Francisco Chronicle had it right: "Two people who love each other should have the chance to build a life together, raising children, sharing dreams and balancing careers."

Predictably, the Yahoos went beserk from their mental caves. They wailed about the sacredness of marriage, lamented ruination of the culture, decried the end of religious faith, declared that marriage was for procreation, labeled homosexuality immoral and damned "activist judges."

Sanctity of marriage? What's so sacred about marriage if one out of two end in divorce?

In dissent, California Justice Marvin Baxter complained that the majority, unsatisfied "with the pace of democratic change...subtitutes, by judicial fiat, its own social policy views for those expressed by the people themselves."

But as Justice Holmes pointed out, courts must act for "the felt necessities" of the times. Chief Justice Warren reinforced that view when he declared that courts must act for fairness and justice.

"Judicial restraint has too often meant judicial abdication of the duty to enforce constitutional guarantees...for too long we have been sweeping under the rug a great many problems basic to American life," Warren said. "We have failed to face up to them."

Leaving public affairs up to the people often produces injustice.

Look no farther than California's "three strikes and you're out" law. Under this reprehensible legislation enacted by the people, some one goes to prison for life for a third felony even if it is as trivial as stealing a bag of golf clubs.

I.F. Stone rightly noted during the 1960s: "If you give power to the people we'd all be in jail."

Under the Justice Baxter rationale, it would have been up to the states to outlaw segregation. But without the Supreme Court's activist role, Alabama and Mississippi still would have apartheid.

The fear here is that a California referendum in November could nullify the humane court decision.

In the federal decision, the court said that the Air Force must prove that Major Margaret Witt's dismissal furthered the military's goals of readiness and cohesion.

The court cited the 2003 Supreme Court decision invalidating the Texas anti-sodomy law as an unconstititional intrusion on privacy.

Witt, a flight nurse, was suspended in 2004 after the Air Force learned that she had a relationship with a civilian. Dismissed in 2007, she filed suit.

But a U.S. district court tossed out her case after the military argued that gays are bad for morale and lead to sexual tension. (Some antediluvians in the Pentagon still argue that homosexuality is a mental disorder.)

Writing a concurrence for the appeals court, Judge Ron Gould noted: "When the government attempts to intrude on the personal and private lives of homosexuals, the government must advance an important interest…and the instrusion must be necessary to further that interest."

An attorney for Witt, James Lobsenz, hailed the appeals court ruling as the beginning of the end for "don't ask, don't tell."

The military policy is so lame. The military fires hundreds of highly capable gay and lesbian soldiers and sailors. It spends millions to recruit and train replacements. It turns down college students who are gay while practically enrolling the lame, the halt and the blind for duty in Iraq.

Social progress in this nation is maddeningly slow. It may take centuries before America is truly civilized. At least the courts are nudging the nation toward civilization.

Sparks Tribune, June 8, 2008

Sensible gun law faces test

Many lobbies besieging Congress are powerful like Big Pharma and the insurance companies. Indeed, the reason America is never likely to have singlepayer, universal health insurance is the drug and insurance firms.

But the Jewish Lobby may be the most potent of all. It is an unspoken rule of American politics that members of Congress never criticize Israeli policies--at least if they hope to be re-elected.

Still another K Street powerhouse not to be crossed is the National Rifle Association. Few members of Congress dare oppose its positions no matter how outrageous they are. But the Supreme Court, whose members have a life term, is beholden to no one. It can vote its politics with impunity.

The court will decide, probably in June, whether the Constitution allows individuals to keep guns in their homes. It also could render a key interpretation of the Second Amendment which declares the "right of the people to keep and bear arms."

The case stems from a Washington, D.C., ordinance banning handguns. The ordinance also requires that guns legally kept in the home, rifles and shotguns, are to be disassembled and/or kept under a trigger lock.

A U.S. appeals court in Washington, contrary to decades of court opinions, declared in March that the ordinance was unconstitutional. It said that the Second Amendment right was an individual one, not linked to service in a militia.

The Supreme Court concluded in 1939 that private ownership of guns must have "some reasonable relationship to the preservation of the efficiency of a well-regulated militia."

The 9th U.S. Circuit Court of Appeals ruled in 1996 that the Second Amendment "does not protect the possession of a weapon by a private citizen." The 6th U.S. Circuit Court of Appeals declared in 1971 that "there can be no serious claim to any express constitutional right of an individual to possess a firearm."

And Chief Justice Warren Burger, by no stretch of the imagination a liberal, called the NRA reading of the Second Amendment, a great fraud, the issue distorted and "confused by calculated disinformation."

The D.C. ordinance, enacted in 1976, is carefully drawn. It is mindful of the needs of citizens to protect themselves from an intruder. The district council members who enacted the ordinance knew that guns allowed at home can be assembled and the trigger unlocked, all in less than a minute.

Colonial days are "ancient" history. So are muskets. Governments today may enact gun curbs such as the D.C. ordinance.

Guns foster the violence rampant in America. The nation records 30,000 gun deaths yearly. Surely government has the right to try to halt some of the slayings. The recent slaughters in Nebraska and Colorado are another in a long line of sickening and senseless killings.

Yet the NRA has constantly stood in the way of sanity. And the Congress has constantly pandered to its agenda. Congress did enact a 10-year ban in 1994 on assault weapons. But when it came up for renewal, President Bush and Congress, caving in to the NRA, allowed the law to lapse.

Roy Romer, former governor of Colorado, summed up the NRA position perfectly when he said: "If the NRA is so out of touch with Colorado that it cannot even support the single proposition that a 14 year old has no business carrying a loaded gun to school, then the NRA is part of the problem not part of the solution."

The NRA *is* part of the problem. When Congress passed a law in 1986 outlawing ownership of machine guns by private citizens, the NRA fought the measure until slapped down by the 5th U.S. Circuit Court of Appeals. (The Supreme Court refused to hear an appeal in the case.)

The NRA, representing the forces of barbarity battling against civilization, has also fought curbs on assault weapons like AK-47s and Uzis. And, yes, the use of armor-piercing bullet. And, yes, it even opposed the Brady Act requiring a five-day waiting period before buying a gun in order to check on felons and the mentally unstable.

Bob Herbert, New York Times columnist, rightly characterizes the NRA as an "inflammatory, obsessive outfit deaf to public opinion." It has "contributed mightily to the long decades of carnage in our streets and homes."

Nevertheless, the Supreme Court, based on its reactionary rulings in the 2006-2007 term, is likely to strike down the D.C. ordinance. If form holds, the American people will be the losers and the NRA the winners yet again.

Sparks Tribune, Dec. 16, 2007

Justices to OK poll tax?

The Republican majority on the highly partisan Supreme Court seems to be poised to approve what amounts to a new poll tax: an Indiana photo identification law.

That certainly was the tenor of the Retrograde Five during oral arguments last month.

Under the Indiana law, voters without photo IDs can cast a provisional ballot. However, the vote is counted only if voters go to the county seat within 10 days to show a photo ID.

Chief Justice Roberts, in effect, asked during oral argument what's the big deal. "County seats aren't very far for people in Indiana," he said.

Yeah. But they *are* far for some voters. For instance, if you don't have a car, it's a 17-mile bus ride to the Lake County seat from Gary, Ind. Whether by car or bus, for most voters it is not worth the bother and expense.

The Supreme Court in 1966 struck down Virginia's poll tax, a Jim Crow measure designed to keep blacks from voting. Justice William O. Douglas, writing the majority opinion, said it was an unconstitutional violation of the Equal Protection Clause of the Fourteenth Amendment. A state cannot make "payment of any fee an election standard," he wrote.

The decision came down in the halcyon days of the great and progressive Warren Court. Now the reactionary Roberts Court seems to think that photo ID is a peachy idea.

Voter ID is an unconstitutional economic standard. The sad truth is that most Republicans favor such laws, laws aimed at keeping Democrats from the polls.

And it is not a case of a just a few people denied the franchise. Estimates are that between 13 million and 22 million Americans of voting age do not have driver's licenses, passports or birth certificates to prove identities. Sometimes it is difficult to obtain birth certificates and can cost as much as $70.

Yet Republican Judge Richard Posner, writing for the 7th U.S. Court of Appeals in Chicago that upheld the Indiana law, said it was such a small burden to get a photo ID.

Untrue. Posner sees the matter from the perspective of too many federal judges: upper class, well-off and conservative. In dissent, appeals Judge Terry Evans had it right: "Let's not beat around the bush. The Indiana voter photo ID law is a not too thinly veiled attempt" to keep Democrats from the polls.

GOP backers of the measure insist that voter fraud is a problem. It is not. No prosecution for impersonating a registered voter has ever been brought.

Yet the Bush administration, always political and often disingenuous about its real ideological motives, is making the issue a Justice Department priority. And note the euphemistic label: voter fraud. It's a solution for a problem that doesn't exist.

So the Bushies adamantly--and fatuously as is so often the case--declare that it is not necessary to wait for fraud to prevent it. "The state's interest in deterring voter fraud before it happens is evident from the monumental harm that can come from such fraud," they claim.

Monumental? Please. Besides, laws should not be made to prevent what *might* happen. They should deal with what *has* happened.

Columnist Cynthia Tucker rightly asks: "Why have leading Republicans invested so much credibility in spreading the canard of widespread election fraud? They use that fiction to push highly restrictive voter ID laws, which tend to block ballot access for poorer black and brown citizens. It's no coincidence that those voters are also more likely to support Democrats."

Richard Hasen, an election law specialist at Loyola law school in Los Angeles, notes sardonically: "There's more than a little bit of irony in going to the Supreme Court and asking it to rise above partisan politics in election cases."

Other states such as Georgia have also enacted photo ID laws. But they are all unconstitutional to any judges or justices who are impartial. The 24th Amendment says so. It is magnificently simple: poll taxes and other taxes to vote are banned. The voter ID is, in effect, a tax.

Yet it is likely that the voter ID law will be upheld. The Supreme Court is so often retrograde. It gave the nation a fraudulent president in 2000 in its worst decision since the proslavery Dred Scott ruling of 1857.

Engraved on the façade of the Supreme Court building are the glowing words: "Equal justice under law." But, like so much inspiring rhetoric in America, it is untrue.

Sparks Tribune, Feb. 10, 2008

5 horsemen of reaction

The Supreme Court has just issued a license to kill by overturning a District of Columbia ban on handguns.

The decision by the third partisan branch of government is as reactionary as it is reprehensible. It embraces the odious position of the National Rifle Association that the Second Amendment protects an individual right to own a gun. It also embraces the terrible violence besmirching America.

A New York Times editorial, rightly denouncing the ruling as "wrong-headed and dangerous," added:

"This is a decision that will cost innocent lives, cause immeasurable pain and suffering and turn America into a more dangerous country. It will also diminsh our standing in the world, sending yet another message that the United States values gun rights over human life."

It was a sad reversal of 70 years of Supreme Court jurisprudence declaring that the Second Amendment restricts the right to bear arms to a militia.

More than 36,000 Americans are shot to death each year while another 65,000 are wounded. Yet Justice Scalia declared that the Constitution does not permit "the absolute prohibition of handguns...used for self-defense in the home."

One reporter, noting that for 22 years Justice Scalia seldom has written an opinion in high profile cases because his views are so far out, called the gun decision his legacy. Some legacy.

Dissenting justices complained about Scalia's reasoning. No wonder. It was irrational. Scalia and the four backward justices who joined his opinion wanted a result and made up reasons to justify it.

In dissent, Justice Stevens called the ruling "strained

and unpersuasive." The majority "would have us believe that more than 200 years ago the Framers made a choice to limit the tools available to elected officials wishing to regulate civilian uses of weapons," Stevens said.

Dissenting Justice Breyer added: "I cannot understand how one can take from the elected branches of government the right to decide whether to insist on a handgun-free urban populace in the city now facing a serious crime problem."

Let's hear no more denunciations of liberal judicial activism. The gun ruling was the quintessence of right-wing judicial activism. But the decision was not surprising coming from the Five Horsemen of Reaction.

The court this term sustained an Indiana voter photo ID law designed by Republicans for Republicans. It struck down the "millionaires amendment" to the federal campaign finance law.

The amendment lifted contribution limits for House of Representative candidates when their opponents spend more than $350,000 of their own money.

But the wealthy justices want the election playing field to be tilted in favor of the rich. The rich have a greater First Amendment than most people.

Justice Stevens rightly dissented, declaring that the amendment sought to reduce "the importance of wealth as a criterion for public office" and to counter "the perception that seats in Congress are available to the wealthiest bidder."

Meanwhile, the court continues to nibble around the death penalty but refuses to abolish it as it should--and civilized countries have. It ruled that the death penalty for child rape violates the Eighth Amendment ban on cruel and unusual punishment.

At least Stevens for the first time said the death penalty is unconstitutional, declaring it "patently excessive and cruel and unusual punishment." Unfortunately, it took him 32 years on the court to reach that wisdom.

In still another sour decision by the Five Horsemen of Reaction, the court reduced a $5 billion punitive damage award against Exxon Mobil to $500 million.

The New York Times editorialized: "This decision invoked a rule that it made up out of whole cloth: that in maritime cases punitive damages should be limited to the amount of compensatory damages."

The numerous 5-4 rulings by the majority of politicians on the court are often made up of legal fictions.

The Exxon case began in 1989 when the supertanker Exxon Valdez hit a reef and spilled 11 million gallons of crude oil into Prince William Sound in Alaska.

Stevens had it right in dissent. He noted that it was irresponsible for Exxon to allow "a lapsed alcoholic" to pilot the ship through treacherous waters, "endangering all of the individuals who depended on the sound for their livelihoods." The jury issued a judgment that expressed its "moral condemnation of Exxon's conduct."

Punitive damages, what the lawyers call "laying on the lash," say: "don't do it again." Unfortunately, the court doesn't want to "lash" its beloved corporations.

This court term illustrates a terrible truth: tyranny of a judicial majority of five in a nation of 305 million.

Sparks Tribune, July 13, 2008

Court's reactionary five

The Supreme Court majority under Chief Justice Roberts has swiftly become the Five Horsemen of Reaction. The five justices are not judges but Republican politicians, every bit as fossilized as the Four Horsemen of Reaction who found New Deal laws unconstitutional.

The Roberts Court ordered resegregation of schools, endorsed sex discrimination, called the First Amendment irrelevant for students, ruled for Big Business and made money talk still louder in politics.

The court condemned race-based enrollment systems in Seattle and Louisville, Ky., toppling the great pillar of the Warren Court, Brown v. Board of Education.

Dissenting Justice Breyer said it was a "cruel distortion of history" for Roberts in his opinion to compare the Seattle and Louisville cases to segregated school districts in the 1950s. Lawyers who worked in the Brown case denounced the decision as "preposterous" and "100 percent wrong."

The Supreme Court was instrumental in rectifying historic wrongs and burying Jim Crow laws. Roberts and his shameful pols have reverted to separate and unequal schools.

Among the court's many other egregious decisions this term was ruling against a woman who was making $6,500 less a year than the lowest paid male supervisor. The court's ruling hinged on a technicality while overturning decades of precedent. The woman in the case, Lilly Ledbetter, did not learn within the required six months that she had been discriminated against.

The court ignored the reality of women in the workplace. As Justice Ginsburg said in dissent: the court "does not comprehend or is indifferent to the insidious way in which women can be victims of pay discrimination."

Or sexual threats. One of Ledbetter's bosses told her:

"If you meet me at the Ramada Inn you can be No. 1. If you don't, you're on the bottom."

The decision was made by five men, the same five--all Catholics--who upheld a horrible law barring late-term abortions. (A far, far better Catholic justice, William Brennan, voted for Roe v. Wade.)

Another repellent decision supported the principal of an Alaskan student suspended because he unfurled a banner declaring "Bong Hits 4 Jesus." Roberts said the student's symbolic speech, as cryptic as it was, encouraged illegal drug use. (Bongs are marijuana water pipes.) Justice Stevens had it right in dissent:

"The court's ham-handed...approach is deaf to the constitutional imperative to permit unfettered debate, even among high school students...inventing out of whole cloth a special First Amendment rule permitting the censorship of any student speech that mentions drugs."

Justice Thomas with his 13th century mind sided with Roberts, as he had in the resegregation case, declaring that students should be denied free speech protection and urged return to the days when "teachers commanded and students obeyed."

Ah, but corporate speech is a different matter. The court ruled that the First Amendment prohibits restrictions on political advertising, upholding the noxious doctrine that money is speech.

In yet another 5-4 vote evincing judicial activism from the Right, the court asked, in effect, what separation of church and state? There is none. The court blocked a lawsuit by a group of atheists and agnostics against the faith-based White House office. The office was created by executive order to give religious charities a share of federal money. You need not be a lawyer to see that as unconstitutional.

Still another outrage: the court overturned an Oregon jury award of $79.5 million in punitive damages against Philip Morris for the harm it caused smokers. It was a victory for corporate wrongdoers whose products have caused widespread injury. It follows a Roberts Court pattern: rule for the powerful over the powerless.

Ohio State law professor, Douglas Berman, made an astute observation after the court refused to grant certiorari in the case of an Arizona man sentenced to 200 years in jail for possessing 20 pornographic pictures of children. Berman pointed out: "Justices think they have a role in regulating extreme corporate punishment but...the court doesn't embrace a role in regulating (excessive) individual punishment."

In still another abhorrent 5-4 ruling in one of the worst terms in Supreme Court history, the court sided with developers against environmentalists.

The biggest disappointment was Justice Kennedy. It had been hoped that he would play the pivotal role of Justice O'Connor. Instead, he joined the reaction of Roberts, Thomas and Justices Scalia and Alito.

President Bush, with his appointment of Roberts and Alito, ruined the Supreme Court just as he has ruined the nation.

The great Justice Louis Brandeis, dissenting in the New State Ice Co. case in 1932, said: "we must be ever on our guard lest we erect our prejudices into legal principles." The Roberts Court has done just that.

Sparks Tribune, July 5, 2007

Bush wrong on speech issue

The Bush administration has been wrong about nearly everything in the past six years.

President Bush sold the Iraq war on lies. He still stubbornly refuses to withdraw from Iraq. He condones torture and outsourcing of torture. He violates the Constitution.

The Bushites fire U.S. attorneys who do not hew to the White House line. They support mountaintop mining in violation of the Clean Water Act. And, among many, many other daily outrages. Bush puts gross incompetents in key positions.

So it is hardly surprising that the Bushites are wrong again on a student free speech issue.

The case, argued before the Supreme Court recently, deals with a high school student who displayed a sign that read, "Bong Hits 4 Jesus," at a 2002 Olympic torch relay in Juneau, Alaska. (Bong hits is slang for using marijuana.)

The 9th U.S. Circuit Court of Appeals correctly ruled that the First Amendment rights of the student, Joseph Frederick, were violated. It cited Tinker as precedent, a 1969 decision declaring that wearing black armbands to school to protest the Vietnam War was symbolic speech deserving constitutional protection.

The Tinker opinion by Justice Abe Fortas said: "It can hardly be argued that either students or teachers shed their constitutional rights to freedom of speech or expression at the schoolhouse gate."

Fortas cited the 1943 ruling in which the court struck down a compulsory flag salute statute in West Virginia: "That they (public schools) are educating the young for citizenship is reason for scrupulous protection of constitutional freedoms of the individual if we are not to strangle the free mind at its source and teach youth to discount important principles of our government as mere platitudes."

Fortas noted that "state-operated schools may not be enclaves of totalitarianism," which they too often are, and proved to be in the Alaska high school case. He added: "Students may not be regarded as closed-circuit recipients of only that which the state chooses to communicate."

The government is trying to make it a drug case, not a free speech matter. It argued, in effect, that the war on drugs takes priority over free speech rights. Kenneth Starr, arguing for the government, said: "Illegal drugs and the glorification of the drug culture are profoundly serious problems for the nation."

Please. A harmless sign glorifies drug usage? The subterfuge is transparent.

Douglas Mertz, who argued the case for the American Civil Liberties Union, was emphatic: "This is not a case about drugs or drug policy. This case is about freedom of speech and teaching our young people the importance of free speech."

The 9th circuit is the most liberal court in the land so it would not be surprising if it is reversed by the reactionary Supreme Court. Indications of that possibility cropped up during oral argument.

Chief Justice Roberts said schools need not tolerate student expression that undermines their educational mission. He asked: "Why is it that the classroom ought to be a forum for political debate simply because the students want to put it on their agenda?"

Answer: because it is essential that every public affairs issue be debated. High schoolers are no exception. Besides, the sign was not displayed in the classroom.

As attorney Mertz pointed out, schools that inculcate an antidrug message must permit students to offer opposing views. He noted that in an open forum, such as the torch parade, it is wrong to tell students that they "may not mention this subject."

Just as the black armbands in Tinker were not disruptive of class, so the sign at the parade disrupted nothing.

Nevertheless, Justice Kennedy argued that the sign was "completely disruptive" of the school's antidrug message. Nonsense. As a letter writer in the New York Times put it: "If a competing thought is disruptive of a fundamentally propagandistic message, that is precisely what the First Amendment was intended to promote and protect."

Even an organization from the religious right, the American Center for Law and Justice, warns that public schools "face a constant temptation to impose a suffocating blanket of political correctness on the educational atmosphere."

Justice Brennan, dissenting in another student free speech case in 1988, said that schools cannot act as "'thought police,' stifling discussion of all but state-approved topics."

Some highly intelligent people of the Right, including the modern guru of conservatism, Bill Buckley, argue for the legalization of all drugs--not just marijuana.

Buckley is right. But even if he is wrong, the student message should be allowed in the marketplace of ideas.

Sparks Tribune, April 5, 2007

Court 'enacts' abortion plank

The five politicians on the Supreme Court have declared, in effect, that abortion is infanticide. President Bush is beaming like the cretin he is over an appalling decision.

A New York Times editorial was dead right: "It comes at a real cost to the court's credibility, its integrity and the rule of law."

The Retrograde Five overturned many excellent lower court rulings. It reversed the Supreme Court's own rule that abortion regulations must have an exception to protect a woman's health.

Three points about the ruling are clear. 1) The law changes with the changing members of the court. 2) The court often decides cases on the basis of its morality rather on that of most people. 3) It is profoundly disturbing that just five justices--all men--make the law for millions about a private matter between a woman and her doctor. (All five are Catholics. A far, far better Catholic justice, William Brennan, voted to support abortion in Roe v. Wade [1973].)

The court recently upheld, 5-4, a moralistic measure passed by a reprehensible Republican Congress. It bore a propagandist title worthy of Goebbels: Partial Birth Abortion Ban Act.

On point one, if Justice Sandra Day O'Connor had still been on the court, it would have been 5-4 the other way. Although a conservative, O'Connor consistently voted pro-choice.

On point two, the Supreme Court refused in 1983 to review lower court rulings upholding firings of two people by a Texas police department simply because of their off-duty cohabitation.

Similarly, in 1977 it refused to grant certiorari when the lower courts upheld the firing of two Pennsylvania library workers because they were living together but unmarried. In neither case was competency in question.

On point three, Justice Kennedy's opinion was patronizing--and absurd. He talked about the "profound respect for the life within the woman." He blathered about the act expressing "the dignity of human life." He blithered about the "ethical and moral concerns." He bleated about "the bond of love that the mother has for her child."

In dissent, Justice Ginsburg, the sole woman on the court, honed in on the long discredited male view. She pointed out that:

• The majority decision was alarming and irrational, the hostility to abortion obvious. Its rationale was flimsy.

• It "tolerates, indeed applauds, federal intervention to ban a procedure found necessary...by the American College of Obstetricians and Gynecologists."

• The court's obligation "is to define the liberty of all, not to mandate (its) own moral code."

• "The court deprives women of the right to make an autonomous choice, even at the expense of safety."

In nonjudicial language, the court ruled "to keep women barefoot and pregnant." But a pro-choice banner has sound advice for government and courts: "butt out of women's lives."

The decision sanctions gross interference by government into medical matters. The barred procedure is often necessary to protect women's health--and even life in case of kidney failure and heart problems.

The ruling is in keeping with the Bush administration's retrograde anti-sex agenda. It opposes abortion, deludes itself about abstinence, tries to block the effective morning-after pill, opposes use of a vaccine to combat cervical cancer and spreads false information about condoms to adolescents.

Tragically, the decision portends Retrograde Five thinking: reversal of Roe. The states keep chipping away at the right to abortion, approving onerous abortion curbs undermining Roe.

•

The numbers are not high for the dilation and extraction abortion at issue in the case, about 2,200 a year. But the principle is everything. Women have an absolute right to abortion, a right to privacy that Justice Harry Blackmun in Roe found in the "penumbras of the Bill of Rights."

As the San Francisco Chronicle wrote: "Millions of American women...have been faced with one of the most difficult decisions of their lives...Doctors should be free to provide them with safe, private care."

Dorothy Samuels, New York Times editorial writer, correctly noted that the court had enshrined "the rhetoric and tactical positioning of the anti-abortion movement." Most notably, she added, the court was using junk science while pretending to act for "for women's own good to protect their mental and moral health."

Clearly, the Supreme Court is marching backward. Even predominantly Catholic countries like Portugal and cities like Mexico City have recently defied the Vatican by legalizing abortion.

Justice Louis Brandeis, perhaps the greatest Supreme Court justice, wrote in a wise dissent: "In the exercise of (our) high power, we must be forever on our guard lest we erect our prejudices into legal principles." The court has done precisely that: turned its prejudices into legal principles.

Sparks Tribune, May 3, 2007

Justice Kennedy pivotal

Fractured. Splintered. Fragmented. Divided. Fissured.

Those words describe the Supreme Court in the 2005-2006 term just ended. More important, the term also confirmed the worst fears of those who opposed the appointments of John Roberts and Samuel Alito: the court grew even more reactionary.

Justice Alito voted with the archconservative Justice Thomas 84 percent of the time in non-unanimous decisions. Chief Justice Roberts sided with another archconservative, Justice Scalia, an amazing 88 percent of the time.

Instead of naming a court after the chief justice as is the custom, it is now the Kennedy Court. Conservative Justice Kennedy has become the swing vote. Because of him, the center sometimes held--precariously. But when Kennedy swings Right, as he often does, the Supreme Court rulings make the law of the land backward.

In its wisest and best decision this term, the court struck down military tribunals. But not much good can be said about the bulk of the rulings.

One of the worst decisions was to invalidate a Vermont statute limiting campaign contributions and spending by candidates. The ruling reaffirmed that money is speech, speech that corrupts the political process. It is nothing less than legalized bribery. It reinforces the fact that America is not the democracy it boasts about. It is a plutocracy.

As Howard Zinn, powerful critic of America past and present, puts it:

"No one can stop us from getting up on a soapbox and speaking our mind. We might reach a hundred people that way. But if we were the Proctor and Gamble Co., which made the soapbox, we could buy prime time for commercials on television, buy full page ads in newspapers and reach several million people.

"Freedom of speech is not simply a yes or no question. It is also a 'how much' question. And how much freedom we have depends on how much money we have."

Another blow to this so-called democracy: the court allowed to stand a mid-decade gerrymander by Texas Republicans. The decision was highly partisan, once again proving that the nonelected justices are mere politicans pretending to be impartial jurists.

Texas had already reapportioned seats after the 2000 census but former majority leader Tom DeLay wanted Republican control of the U.S. House so he pushed through another reapportionment. The court's rationale, partisan legerdemain so transparent that even a magician would be ashamed to use it, tore up the due process clause of the Constitution.

The reapportionment illegally reduced black and Latino voting strength. But no matter. Political appointees at the Justice Department overruled six lawyers and two analyists who called the plan invalid.

Another horrible decision decided by the Reactionary Five restricted free speech rights of 21 million public employees, declaring that the First Amendment does not protect them from complaints to their bosses about wrongdoing.

It was vicious slap at government whistle-blowers--truth-tellers--who expose corruption and fraud. Justice Souter, dissenting, said the "public interest in addressing wrongdoing and threats to health and safety" is paramount. And Justice Stevens noted in dissent the perversity of protecting whistle-blowers who go public while punishing in-house speech.

On wetlands, the fragmented court was unable to decide on the scope of the Clean Water Act. But Justice

Stevens rightly pointed out that the retrograde bloc--Roberts, Scalia, Thomas and Alito--was "antagonistic to environmentalism" and "needlessly jeopardized the quality of our water." Stevens also noted that the bloc was making law rather than interpreting it, a dig at conservatives who accuse liberal judges of judical activism.

All decisions, however, were not bad. The Supreme Court ruled that the Justice Department does not have the authority to block Oregon's physician-assisted suicide and that federal narcotics law cannot stop a religious sect from importing a hallucinogenic tea central to its worship.

Roberts, in a unanimous opinion for the court, noted that for the past 35 years the government has permitted Native Americans to use peyote in religious rituals even though it is banned for general use.

Nevertheless, a look at Roberts' first term reveals mostly dread news. He dissented in the death-with-dignity case. He dissented in the wetlands case, siding with developers. He voted with those who approved the money-is-speech decision. He voted with those who upheld shameful gerrymandering. He voted to deny whistle-blowing rights, declaring that he could find no First Amendment injury even when a whistle-blower was demoted for speaking out.

Reaction is firmly in the saddle. The great fear about future high court rulings: the liberating abortion decision of Roe v. Wade in 1973 will be overturned.

                              Sparks Tribune, July 27, 2006

Court tilts toward Business

Too many Americans mistakenly revere the U.S. Supreme Court. They think it is an impartial body juxtaposing the texts of laws with the Constitution to determine constitutionality.

Alas, it is not so. The court is as political as the Republican and Democratic parties. Supreme Court justices are Republicans or Democrats even though they no longer bear such labels.

This is evident in their decisions, decisions cloaked in the majesty of the law: deep, lawyerly, double-domed. Oral arguments usually indicate how the "politicians" will vote.

So it was during oral arguments recently on global warming. Comments of the justices indicated that the court is divided, 4-4, four "Republicans" against four "Democrats" even though two of the "Democrats" were appointed by GOP presidents.

Key to the outcome in the case is Justice Anthony Kennedy. His vote will probably decide whether it is 5-4 in favor of liberalism or 5-4 in favor of reaction.

Specifically, the case turns on the question: does the Clean Air Act require the Environmental Protection Agency to impose limits on greenhouse gas emissions?

The Bush adminstration, always siding with Business rather than the health and welfare of people, says no. (White House lawyers are working hand-in-glove with the auto industry, which says it all.)

However, the attorney general in Massachusetts says yes, calling it the most pressing environmental case in decades. He adds: "The indisputable fact in this case is that our climate is changing and that change is being caused by dangerous greenhouse gas emissions."

Justice Stevens noted during oral argument that the EPA ignored key findings from the National Academy of Science report on global warming. "In their selective quotations they left out parts that indicated far less uncertainty than the agency purported to find," he said.

The San Francisco Chronicle can also see the matter quite clearly: "Melting glaciers, worsening smog, droughts and stronger hurricanes are evidence."

Sen. Ted Kennedy is aware of the politics of this "nonpartisan" court. He pointed out that Chief Justice Roberts and Justice Alito last term "consistently voted to erode civil liberties, decrease the rights of minorities and limit protections...They voted to expand the power of the president, reduce restrictions on abusive police tactics and approve federal intrusion into issues traditionally governed by state law."

So it is on the environment. Roberts and Alito naturally side with Business on environmental matters. Their thinking was exemplified earlier this year when they joined a court opinion describing wetlands as mere "transitory puddles."

Meanwhile, nothing is sacred to the Bush mob, not even the splendors of the great national parks in the West.

The mobsters have politicized and trashed a priceless heritage for generation, after generation, after geneanation. It is a terrible indictment of a terrible president who robs all Americans--Republicans, Democrats and nonpartisans--of magnificent treasures.

The Bushites allow snowmobiles in Yellowstone National Park, belching smoke, polluting the winter wonderland and shattering the peace and quiet. They are masters of the Orwellian euphemism of "war is peace." Thus we have a "Healthy Forest Act" that is destructive and a "Clear Skies Act" that promotes pollution.

Orwell in his essay, "Politics and the English Language," notes that political language "is designed to make lies sound truthful and murder respectable."

A blistering article in Z magazine last summer noted how the Bush administration has systematically enfeebled the environmental protection laws, "appointing industry lobbyists, changing or ignoring rules and enforcement, and passing new laws to negate protections."

Bush and his wrecking crew rolled back more than 300 regulations. Z reports: "The administration encouraged loggers, developers, snowmobilers and property rights advocates to sue the government to overturn environmental regulation. Meanwhile, the Justice Department defends environment laws in language clearly intended to weaken them."

EPA is so blatantly politicized that ideology is everything and science nothing. Sen. Frank Lautenberg of New Jersey notes: "the administration has effectively declared war on science and truth to advance its anti-environment agenda...It continues to censor scientists who have documented the impacts of global warming."

The EPA rejected the recommendations of its own staff scientists and scientific advisory council to tighten standards of regulating soot. Why? To save power companies and industrial polluters nearly $2 billion by not installing new equipment.

Never mind, as the New York Times points out, that the tougher standards could save 24,000 lives and $50 billion annually in health care costs.

In the Bush administration, money is everything, people are nothing. Will America ever be wise enough to vote out grasping and ruthless capitalism for benevolent and humane socialism?

Sparks Tribune, Dec. 14, 2006

Court rebukes King Bush

I, my Lords, embody the Law
"Iolanthe"
by W.S. Gilbert

The Supreme Court has grown even more reactionary with the replacement of Sandra Day O'Connor by Samuel Alito. But even such a retrograde court refuses to let President Bush make the law.

The court recently struck down military commissions established by Bush to try prisoners at Guantánamo. It ruled that the tribunals were unauthorized by Congress and violated international law.

"The executive is bound to comply with the rule of law," Justice Stevens wrote in a 5-3 plurality decision. He said military tribunals do not afford "all the judicial guarantees that are recognized as indispensable for civilized peoples." These guarantees include prohibition of coerced testimony, torture, beatings, sexual assault and religious humiliation.

Stevens quoted James Madison, father of the Constitution, approvingly: "The accumulation of all powers, legislative, executive and judiciary, in the same hands...may justly be pronounced the very definition of tyranny."

At Guantánamo you have such travesties of justice as: no legal counsel, testimony without oath, hearsay evidence, defendants excluded from hearings, and unsworn testimony. Above all, prisoners are held indefinitely, without charges and without trial.

Star Chamber proceedings in the 21st century.

Precedent for the tribunal ruling comes from some of the wisest opinions ever written by Supreme Court justices. Namely:

- Chief Justice John Marshall, presiding at the treason trial of Aaron Burr in 1807, ruled that the president, unlike the king of England, is not above the law.
- Justice Frank Murphy, dissenting in In Re Yamashita (1946): "We live under the Constitution, which is the embodiment of all the high hopes and aspirations of the new world. And it is applicable in war and peace."
- Justice Robert Jackson, concurring in a court decision to block an attempt by President Truman to seize the steel mills in 1952, said the president acted unconstitutionally because Congress had refused to authorize the seizure. The court ruled 6-3 against Truman.
- Chief Justice Warren Burger, writing for a unanimous court in the Nixon tapes case (1974), cited the nation's "historic commitment to a rule of law." He quoted Marshall in Marbury v. Madison (1803): " 'it is emphatically the province and duty of the judicial department to say what the law is.' "

The historic Hamdan tribunal decision was a sharp rebuke to Bush, a denunciation of a kangaroo court and usurpation of power.

The Bush administration is riddled with other above-the-law practices: illegal wiretapping of Americans by the National Security Agency, kidnappings to send captives abroad for torture, and bill-signing statements to interpret the law as Bush defines it.

The administration goes its own nefarious way, the public and Congress be damned. A year ago the Senate voted, 90-9, to ban "cruel, inhumane and degrading treatment of prisoners." (Vice President Cheney objected strenuously. Presumably he favors summary execution.) But the Senate vote had no effect on an administration run amok.

In dissent, the rebarbative Justice Thomas said the Hamdan ruling "flouts our well-established duty to respect the executive judgment in matters of military operation and foreign affairs."

Thomas woefully misplaces his trust. Bush is unworthy of trust. Justices have no duty to obey a lying president. It is not traitorous to disagree with a president acting like a king.

Another rebarative justice is Scalia. In dissent, he dismissed as crazy the notion that military detainees are entitled to a "full jury trial." He scoffs at the idea that the Geneva Conventions apply to those held at Guantánimo. He despises thinking by foreign jurists even though America is increasingly out of step with international law.

Scalia uttered prejudicial comments before the Hamdan case was argued but refused to recuse himself. He is an "original intent" interpreter of the Constitution who has no truck with the dictum of Justice Holmes that the law must respond to the "felt necessities" of the day. (Oh, and Scalia says U.S. institutions come from God.)

The dissenters are rubber-stamping anything Bush does even if it is autocratic, monarchial, plenary and unitary.

Every high school student learns about the checks and balances in the U.S. political process. How the Congress passes bills, the president vetoes bills, how vetoes can be overridden and the Supreme Court determines constitutionality.

But Bush has made it clear that checks and balance are for textbooks. The law is what he says it is.

Sparks Tribune, July 20, 2006

Worst
Supreme Court Decisions

Outrageous Rulings

The problem with the Supreme Court is that the justices are lawyers.

That is not a joke from a late night TV show. It's a searing truth.

Lawyers are legalistic rather than humanistic. They are narrow-minded rather than broad-minded. They "follow the law" of yesteryear rather than meet the problems of today.

They favor corporations rather than consumers. They tend to be conservative personally and pragmatically. You don't get ahead in the legal fraternity by being a radical.

Most federal judges are rich. In two terms, President Reagan appointed 279 U.S. judges. The majority each had a net worth of $400,000. One fifth of them were millionaires. Such judges are unlikely to see things from the perspective of ordinary people.

Most justices have been mediocrities. President Washington named 10 justices, "a thoroughly undistinguished lot," Peter Irons wrote in "A People's History of the Supreme Court."

President Truman named three former Senate buddies who were out of their depth on the court. President Kennedy, a so-called liberal, appointed a conservative to the court because he was his Colorado campaign manager.

Many court members had just one qualification: they were corporate power attorneys.

Yet such people decide the law of the land. As Chief Justice Charles Hughes knew so well: "The Constitution is what the judges say it is." Often what the justices "say it is" has been bad.

The justices were still "nine old men" even after Justice Sandra Day O'Connor became the first woman on the court in 1981. As the great socialist leader Eugene Debs pointed out, a member of the working class has never been on the federal bench let alone on the august Supreme Court.

The Supreme Court's best justice, Louis Brandeis, was called the "people's lawyer" before joining the top court in 1916 where he became the "people's justice." But most justices have been retrograde. They retarded progress rather than stretched the legal frontiers. The corporations have the money, working people do not. Lawyers go where the money is.

Chief Justice John Roberts is a former corporate lawyer in Washington who made $1 million a year. So it was natural the Roberts Court became a Corporate Court.

In the 2009-2010 term, it took the side of the U.S. Chamber of Commerce in 13 out of 16 cases, including the infamous Citizens United decision which declared money speech and corporations people. (The New Yorker had a wonderful cartoon about Citizen United. Paraphrasing "Merchant of Venice," a lawyer pleads before the justices: "If you prick a corporation, does it not bleed? If you tickle it, does it not laugh? If you poison it, does it not die?")

In the 2010-2011 term, the Roberts Court cut down an exemplary Arizona statute that leveled the financial playing field, rejected a suit by 1.6 million women against a woefully discriminatory Wal-Mart, shielded the makers of drugs from lawsuits by patients who had been harmed, smothered lawsuits against mutual fund cheaters and liars, and disallowed a suit by a death row inmate even though the prosecution failed to turn over exculpating evidence.

The Supreme Court has had 112 justices and chief justices in its history, about 15 of them liberal to progressive.

They were justices like William Johnson (1804-1834), Samuel Miller (1862-1890), John Harlan I (1877-1911), Louis Brandeis (1916-1939), Oliver Wendell Holmes (1902-1932), Harlan Stone (1925-1941), Benjamin Cardozo (1932-1938), Hugo Black (1937-1971), William

O. Douglas (1939-1975), Frank Murphy (1940-1949), Robert Jackson (1941-1954), Earl Warren (1953-1969), William Brennan (1956-1990), Thurgood Marshall (1967-1991) and John Paul Stevens (1975-2010).

The worst decision the Supreme Court ever made was Dred Scott in 1857, upholding the obnoxious Fugitive Slave Act. The language of Chief Justice Roger B. Taney was atrocious coming from anyone—let alone a member of the Supreme Court. It was beyond racism, totally devoid of humanity.

Blacks were "an inferior order and altogether unfit to associate with the white race," Taney wrote. "They had no rights that the white man was bound to respect."

Moreover: "The Negro might justly and lawfully be reduced to slavery for his own benefit." They were not citizens and could not claim the "rights and privileges" of citizenship even if their masters took them to free states.

In the second worst ruling, the Supreme Court in 2000 declared G.W. Bush president although Al Gore got 543,895 more votes. Just five people out of 280 million Americans engineered the coup. The court stopped the vote count in Florida, in defiance of their usual deference to states' rights, and gave Bush the Electoral College victory.

Vincent Bugliosi in The Nation wrote angrily that the court "committed one of the biggest and most serious crimes that the nation has ever seen—pure and simple theft of the presidency."

The Felonious Five stole the election under the color of law.

Justices are adept at making up reasons to support their predilections. But in this case, the sophistry was incredible.

The five, all Republicans, rendered a totally partisan decision. It gave no rationale, no analysis. It did not cite a single case or precedent.

It suppressed the facts. The unsigned opinion was

convoluted and opaque. Then, like the thieves they were, the unjust justices vanished shamefully into the night.

In the third worse decision, Citizens United (2010), the court reaffirmed earlier declarations that money is speech.

Democracy had already been corrupted with legalized bribery in the form of campaign contributions. But with Citizens United, the New York Times exploded: "The Supreme Court has thrust politics back to the Robber Baron era of the 19th century. Disingenuously waving the flag of the First Amendment, the court's majority has paved the way for corporations to use their vast treasuries to win elections."

Historian Howard Zinn put the matter in perspective: "No one can stop us from getting on a soapbox and speaking. We might reach 100 people that way. But if we were Proctor and Gamble, which makes the soapbox, we could buy prime time for TV commercials and buy full-page ads in newspapers, reaching several million. How much freedom we have depends on how much money we have."

In the fourth worse ruling, *Plessy v. Ferguson* (1896), the court upheld Southern apartheid, declaring separate black and white facilities constitutional. Justice Harlan I dissented, calling the Constitution color-blind. It took 58 years for the Supreme Court to declare Harlan right.

The fifth worse decision was *Santa Clara County v. Southern Pacific Railroad* (1886). The court declared that corporations were people and entitled to constitutional rights even though the preamble of the Constitution starts with "we the people."

The sixth worst ruling, *Lochner v. New York* (1905), reversed a legislative limit of a 10-hour work day and 60-hour work week for bakers. Justice Rufus Peckham, writing for a 5-4 majority, outrageously declared that such statutes "limiting the hours in which grown and intelligent men may labor to earn their living are mere meddlesome interference with the rights of the individual."

Justice Harlan I dissented, rightly complaining that employer and employee are not on equal footing. Bosses have the upper hand. Always have. Always will.

In another Lochner dissent, Holmes pointed out: "This case is decided on an economic theory that a large part of the country does not entertain. The 14th Amendment does not enact Mr. Herbert Spencer's Social Statics." (Spencer was a Social Darwinist.)

In the seventh worst ruling, the Supreme Court in 2000 upheld the right of Big Tobacco to advertise cigarettes, a product that kills 500,000 Americans yearly. Corporate freedom and the merchants of death prevailed over the health of Americans.

Cigarettes are a drug. Federal Judge Jerome Frank, dissenting in a 1941 case, wrote: "Such men as Paine, Milton and Jefferson were not fighting for the right to peddle commercial advertising." True. But the Supreme Court is often blind to truth.

In the eighth worst decision, the Supreme Court in 1895 struck down a congressional income tax law. The vote was 5-4, five wealthy justices killing it as a scholar's chart demonstrated.

In the ninth worse ruling, the court in Schenck (1919) ruled that harmless leaflets were a "clear and present danger" to national security under the 1917 Espionage Act. The absurdity was manifest. Yet ever since the court nearly always has taken the side of so-called national security.

Indeed, the Obama administration, far from being receptive to whistle-blowers as it promised in 2008, is still using the bogus Espionage Act to prosecute and persecute leakers like Pfc. Bradley Manning.

The U.S. government detests leakers because they reveal embarrassing truths. That's why federal prosecutors have drawn up a sealed indictment—secret charges—against Julian Assange, WikiLeaks founder.

David Carr, media critic of the New York Times, calls the Espionage Act an "ad hoc Official Secrets Act, which is not a law that has ever found traction in America. The people's right to know is viewed as superceding the government's right to hide its business."

In the 10th worse decision, *Adkins v. Children's Hospital* (1923), the court invalidated a minimum wage for women workers in the District of Columbia. Justice George Sutherland, one of the Four Horseman of Reaction writing for the majority, said it was "simply and exclusively a price-fixing law." In dissent, Chief Justice William Taft pointed out that employees "are particularly subject to the overreaching of the harsh and greedy employer."

The rankings are debatable. Selecting the 10 worst decisions out of thousands of Supreme Court rulings in history is difficult. As Justice John Harlan II remarked in an obscenity case: "One man's vulgarity is another's lyric."

But there is no question of the pro-business bias and horrible rulings—and non-rulings—of the court historically.

The court steadfastly refused to enforce constitutional amendments—13, 14 and 15—and allowed Jim Crow to continue in the South 125 years after the Civil War. (The 13th freed the slaves, the 14th made them citizens and the 15th entitled them to vote.) From 1880 to 1937, historian Henry Steele Commager noted, "the political field was strewn with the corpses of social welfare laws struck down by judicial weapons." The court overturned minimum-wage laws, workers' compensation statutes, utility regulations and child labor laws.

The justices in those cases raised anguished cries of "freedom of contract!" They demanded a "halt to the march of communism!" In the early 1930s, the Four Horsemen of Reaction repealed the Roosevelt New Deal.

"The business of America is business," President Coolidge boasted. Unfortunately, the "Supremes" so often have agreed.

Justice Samuel Miller, Iowan who served from 1862 to 1890, summed up the problem of having the Supreme Court bulging with lawyers:

"It is vain to contend with judges who have been, at the bar, the advocates of railroad companies and all the forms of associated capital when they are called on to decide cases where such issues are in contest. All their training, all their feelings, are from the start in favor of those who need no such influence."

And that is precisely why Earl Warren was the greatest chief justice. He put people over property, human needs over the money-making demands of capitalism. Chief Justice John Marshall (1801-1835) put property over people. (He said that slaves were mere property.) Warren defied the conservative image of far too many attorneys.

Reno News & Review, March 8, 2012

Magnificent Dissents

Magnificent dissents

Despite the long litany of woes heaped on the people by the court majority over 224 years, some great dissents have illustrated what it means to be an American. It does not mean wearing a flag pin or flying flags on pickup trucks.

It means dissents as In re Yamashita (1946). The court upheld the hanging of a Japanese general ordered by a military commission, declaring that the findings of a military panel were unreviewable. Justice Murphy dissented because the general was denied due process and a fair trial.

"No exception is made to those who are accused of war crimes or those who possess the status of an enemy belligerent. Indeed, such an exception would be contrary to the whole philosophy of human rights which makes the Constitution the great living document that it is.

"The immutable rights of the individual belong not alone to the members of those nations that excel on the battlefield or that subscribe to democratic ideology. They belong to every person in the world, victor or vanquished, whatever may be his race, color or beliefs. They rise above every status or outlawry. They survive any popular passion or frenzy of the moment.

"While people in other lands may not share our beliefs as to due process and the dignity of the individual, we are not free to give effect to our emotions in recklesss disregard or the rights of others. We live under a Constitution which is the embodiment of all the high hopes and aspirations of the new world."

In Olmstead (1928) the court upheld wiretapping but Holmes and Brandeis dissented. Holmes declared it would be better for "some criminals to escape than that the government should play an ignoble part."

Brandeis in his dissent declared: "The makers of our Constitution undertook to secure conditions favourable to the pursuit of happiness....They conferred, as against the government, the right to be let alone—the most comprehensive of rights and the right most valued by civilized men...Our government is the potent, the omnipresent teacher. It teaches the whole people by its example. If the government becomes a lawbreaker it breeds contempt for the law."

After his disastrous ruling in Schenck, Holmes came to his senses with a marvelous dissent six months later in Abrams (1919). He deplored the 20-year prison sentence for publishing two harmless leaflets. He pointed out that the defendants were punished "not for what the indictment alleges but for the creed that they avow."

He concluded with a ringing declaration of free speech: "We should be eternally vigilant against any attempts to check the expression of opinions that we loathe."

Justice Harlan Stone was the sole dissenter in Gobitis (1940) when the court upheld a school flag-salute statute. The Jehovah's Witnesses objected because to them saluting the flag was worshiping a graven image.

"It is a long step, and one which I am unable to take, to the position that government may, as a supposed educational measure, compel public affirmations which violate religious conscience," Stone wrote.

"The very essence of liberty is the freedom of the individual from compulsion as to what he shall think and what he shall say. This seems to me no more than the surrender of the constitutional protection of the liberty of small minorities to the popular will."

Stone was proved right just three years later in Barnette when Justice Jackson made his great statement about the Bill of Rights: "The very purpose of a Bill of Rights was to withdraw certain subjects from the vicissitudes of political controversy, to place them beyond the reach of majorities and officials and to establish them as legal principles to be applied by the courts.

"One's right to life, liberty and property, to free speech, a free press, freedom of worship and assembly may not be submitted to a vote. They depend on the outcome of no elections."

In Zorach v. Clauson (1952) the court upheld a New York public school board policy of allowing students released time to attend religious classes. Justice Douglas, to his everlasting shame, wrote the majority opinion. "We are a religious people whose institutions presuppose a Supreme Being," he wrote.

In a sizzling dissent, Justice Jackson answered Douglas:

• "The day that this country ceases to be free for irreligion it will cease to be free for religion."

• "The wall which the court was professing to erect between church and state has become even more warped and twisted than I expected."

• "Today's judgment will be more interesting to students of psychology and of the judicial processes than to students of constitutional law."

It is dissents like these that should make Americans proud.

Reno News & Review, March 8, 2012

www.ingramcontent.com/pod-product-compliance
Lightning Source LLC
Chambersburg PA
CBHW030444300426
44112CB00009B/1155